# SWIMMING FREE

On and Below the Surface of
Lake, River and Sea

Geoffrey Fraser Dutton

# SWIMMING FREE

On and Below the Surface of
Lake, River and Sea

Dh'iarr a' mhuir a bhith 'ga tadhal
*The sea asked to be visited*—Traditional

ST. MARTIN'S PRESS, NEW YORK

AFFILIATED PUBLISHERS: Macmillan & Company, Limited,
London—also at Bombay, Calcutta, Madras and Melbourne—
The Macmillan Company of Canada, Limited, Toronto

# CONTENTS

Illustrations between pages 58 and 59

# 1
## About this book

What can we do with ourselves—what is there to do—once we have learnt to swim? I hope to answer this question in the following pages. I hope to show that there exists for every swimmer a new and unsuspected world—not thousands of miles away or hugely expensive but here under his nose in river, lake, sea, even in pond and ditch and flooded meadow, available *now* with the simplest of equipment. You no longer have to brave frigid waters—warm rubber suits are for all; with fins and mask and snorkel you enjoy a confidence and freedom of the water never before offered to Man. You merely need to be a competent swimmer, sound in mind and body. You merely need to have learnt to swim—well. Then you can begin to look around you, at your new inheritance.

I offer in these pages a personal solution—but it applies to everyone who longs to explore aquatic worlds more imaginative than a swimming pool, and more accessible than the Red Sea; and who wishes simply to swim, and not be burdened with expensive specialized apparatus. It should whet the appetite of those who are not yet competent swimmers, and refresh those who are happy just to be beside loch, river or sea—everyone, surely, who finds that adventure in our despoiled terrestrial environment becomes ever less satisfying and ever more mechanical. Here is simplicity and freedom, uncontaminated, unsuspected.

Think of the situation if hill-walking or even rambling was considered quite impractical and all our exercise had to be taken in gymnasia, with outdoor enjoyment restricted to severe Alpine faces or remote Himalayan peaks. . . . Yet how few of us imagine any sort of swimming other than round bathing pools or beaches on the one hand and down the esoteric depths of aqualung diving on the other. How few of us know the thrill and power of kicking free from tide and current, of twisting in a moment beneath white foam into cool, rich shadows that glow with amber and olive and gold, or of drifting and rolling, and plunging and rising, and drifting again; how few know of this freedom of the intricate tapestried depths and of the miles of glittering surface, among the sunlit rock-visiting waves. How few know what to do with themselves, once they have learnt to swim.

The question is a highly relevant one today. All over the suburban world, children are being taught to keep afloat and move themselves in the water. How do they use their new competence? In the countries of the British Isles almost everyone under the age of twenty-five is now able to swim, and possesses some dusty certificate or other awarded him years ago when he climbed out happy and dripping after the statutory number of lengths: yet how many people do you see *really* swimming? By the sea, by rivers and lakes, there is much splashing and intermittent bobbing, but how few heads are swimming any distance, and how rarely—along rocky shores or sandy beaches, in the pools beneath waterfalls, across the silence of lakes—how rarely in these places do you meet a human being simply swimming, hour after hour on and below the surface, at home in this other environment, free in the golden or the silver mirror.

Presumably, therefore, most of us who learn to swim do so in case we fall in. One of the most satisfying pursuits is limited to saving a dry skin upset from various complicated activities above the water such as sailing, canoeing or waterskiing; to save it so that it can as rapidly as possible scramble back upon its planks or its earth. Being able to swim, for most of us, means that immersion is no longer a disaster, but an inconvenience. The 'certificate' admits us to apparently more enjoyable pastimes in which the water is secondary; we use only its surface, and travel across that on wood or fibreglass or metal. Swimming has been learnt, not from love of the water, but from fear of it.

A few people do seem to like water as water, for they continue to swim; but mostly in swimming baths. There the inbuilt constraints, mental and physical, keep us from full sympathy with the water. Such crowded exercise yards only offer us joys of speed or style; even the larger ones are as desolate of further delight as are barrack squares. Yet so often they are accepted as the ultimate arena. Competition after competition lashes their surface, participants hurling themselves, in foam of chlorine and detergent, from wall to wall and back again. The water is still secondary; and one's companions no more than competitors.

We must not condemn swimming baths. They are useful to learn and practise in, and can be fun. But do we have to stay in them? Once we've learnt to walk and run we don't race about the school playground for the rest of our lives, or pant obsessively between white lines on cinders. We go out on to the fields, the hills; ramble, climb, laze on summits in the sun, race—if you wish—downhill or uphill, but spontaneously, as part of the mastery and enjoyment of our limbs.

Why, then, when we have gained similar mastery in the water, don't we equally well go down to the shores of river, lake or sea and swim out there, exploring this other world (after all, the greater part of our planet), enjoying the water in its own right and entering it alert and ready to learn? Why shut ourselves up in the gymnasium? Outside wait the great Atlantic forests, the sombre trout-haunted pools, the green and gold rivers flashing with salmon, the rough and tumble of waterfalls, the great lift and roll of endless ridge-breaking waves, the moon-rippled silence of empty lakes.

We complain of our disappearing landscape, but this vast waterscape awaits us scarcely touched. Why seek out Greenland or the Andes or the Moon to sharpen ourselves against an unpredictable environment, to discover ourselves as human beings? The challenge surrounds us here. We can find in the water satisfactions no longer offered us by today's ration of land and its sooted mouthfuls of air—or indeed by any terrestrial existence, however unpolluted.

These satisfactions, though just round the corner, cannot be guessed at by those who have achieved their certificate and then clambered out gratefully to a future of dry land. The gulf between the aquatic world of their experience and that of Captain Cousteau is so wide they accept it with complacency. They can hardly be blamed for believing themselves permanently under-privileged, for ever captive spectators. The local public baths certainly offer them no hint of swimming as an immediately realizable adventure, and where else can they think to go? In most of Europe and the United States people live in congested urban areas. Any 'wild' water there is pestiferous or poisoned. They have no choice but to visit artificial water except on holidays, and then the favourite shores are usually so churned and clouded by countless feet that lying in the sun is preferable. Most people will find it very hard at first to break away from artificial water.

Surely, therefore, we should devise more satisfying artificial waters than the present swimming pools, places where we can enjoy our painfully acquired skill and become easy in the water, savouring its different moods on the surface and below. Then we might more willingly graduate to the seas and rivers.

At the end of this book I have sketched a possible design for such a pool, on the lines of an aquatic park. Swimmers educated there might expect to find further pleasures in wild waters—even in those of our own islands. For, as I have suggested, most people believe that scenes of great underwater beauty and power exist only in localities as romantic and relatively inaccessible as the Red Sea, the Barrier Reef or, more suburbanly, the Mediterranean, and out there are only available to those skilled in the craft of Cousteau and Hass: those who, gleaming with dials and cylinders and floodlights, sink to remote, sophisticated depths. This is nonsense. I hope in this book to present some experiences which, I find, rival and sometimes excel those in exotic waters; and such experiences are waiting here for any competent swimmer.

I hope also to suggest that the usual excuses put forward against such pleasure in our waters—that they are too dangerous, too cold, too boring, too difficult to see in—no longer hold today with the advent of mask, fins and simple

4

protective clothing. Our waters are not too dangerous for a competent sensible swimmer with fins and snorkel and mask; in a cheap neoprene suit he can swim among ice and be warm, drift the roughest seas and not sink; no water is boring to such a swimmer, for his senses are always being challenged or flattered; and even the murkiest river has its ceaseless procession of surface pleasures.

But I must make clear at this beginning that I write on two separable planes—one a fairly objective illustration that touring, or 'adventure', swimming is not only enjoyable but perfectly safe and possible here provided certain conditions are fulfilled; the other, quite subjective, is an account of my own response to such swimming and need not—in some instances should certainly not—be held as a precedent to follow. For example, common sense should ensure that you do not venture far out, or for long, alone; yet I find the subtler pleasure and greater reward come to the solitary swimmer. If I were writing a text book on this wider swimming (which I assuredly am not) I would pronounce that one should never swim alone; nevertheless I often swim alone and in this book describe many solitary excursions. It is a question of skill, experience and personality. The analogy with wandering among the hills is complete. Clearly it is safer to go with a group; equally obviously the hills yield more to the solitary climber. Difficulties are sought—one's horizon is stretched always a little further—but the accompanying dangers are reduced to a minimum by craft and skill. Acquiring such proficiency and thereby overcoming ever greater difficulties with the least exposure to objective danger, permits the traveller—on hill or in water—to perfect his relationship with a little more of this earth and so to comprehend it, and perhaps himself, somewhat better. Naturally, dangers will still exist. If you do not wish to meet and understand them, stay at home or in town, fight your own battles there against virus and motorcar; but do not lecture those who take their gift of muscle and brain to a different testing ground.

Let me emphasize this subject of safety: it is better to be accused of repetition than of preaching foolhardiness. Until

5

some hundred and fifty years ago it was considered highly dangerous to walk among hills, let alone high mountains; only intrepid hunters or shepherds, by some inherited strength or intuition, could appear to do so without swift disaster. Nowadays tens of thousands, in the British Isles alone, walk the hills safely in all weathers. As social changes habituated us to exploration, the 'impossibly dangerous' hills became merely 'hazardous' and then 'perfectly safe provided reasonable precautions are taken'. Of course there will always be the idiots or the unbalanced who do not take the precautions the rest of us understand, in the hills as in lighting the gas cooker, and they suffer the consequences; but we do not all stay on the flat or eat cold suppers because of them. The hills are now accepted, and books about exploring hills, collecting hills or watching birds among hills pour from the presses uncounted and uncriticized. The swimming I describe in this book is not yet familiar. The waters, to some people on the brink, must appear 'impossibly dangerous', their risks incalculable. If you believe that, then to swim there would certainly be irresponsible. To others, good swimmers perhaps, intoxicated with their new fins, every tide-race now appears 'perfectly safe'; they, too, are irresponsible. All water is dangerous, and will remain so until we develop gills. But my point is to emphasize that a sensible mean operates between the quaverers and the plungers: the sensible mean that forbids us to wear shorts on the Cairngorms in October, that turns us back on Crib Goch in smooth leather soles, that switches the gas oven on *after* we have lit the match. I depend on that sensible mean throughout this book, where the dangers are presented as well as the safety. These dangers in swimming free, as in crossing Times Square, must be recognized. Once recognized, the prudent may avoid them; the adventurous may learn to outwit them; the fools, alas—and without Cuchulainn's excuse—fight the waves, and drown; if they have not already been extinguished by a blizzard, or a taxi-driver, or a gas explosion. Of course the adventurous, and even the prudent, can also drown, through an act of God like a heart attack or a tidal wave or through a simple mistake (who has not at least once forgotten to look both ways before crossing the road?); but let us not confuse these genuine accidents with disasters wilfully brought about.

This is a book of exploration, of the surface and of what lies beneath, and of the exploring animal itself as it enters its ancient, hardly remembered home. The book, as a book, is also an exploration. Much has been written on swimming, much on deep diving, but little from the viewpoint of the swimmer who, alone or with a distant companion, floats masked and finned, wrestling with his double vision: a vision above and below his surface, of sea and shore, of his land life and his new water life, of his old acquiescence and the present revelation. I will try, as faithfully as I can, to record my impressions of a state which all experience who dive and swim long distances and which explains their dedication, their addiction, to this pursuit. It is a sport, a way of life, as compelling and educative as mountaineering, that great adventure on land, and one may expect any account of it to suffer the weaknesses familiar in mountaineering literature. One may pardon, therefore, the gaucherie, the overemphases, the transcendentalism, which must mar these pages; we are still at the adolescence of free swimming as a sport, still in the Alps before 1854, and a little overmuch enthusiasm, a sincere if clumsy mysticism, may be excused in this Golden Age. No one has been here before; the waters are undisturbed, and the clichés scarcely fingered.

I am conscious, too, of much anthropomorphism in the descriptions; but to me this quality is characteristic of the bright and primitive underwater vision, and to edit these recollections with a terrestrial knowingness is to break faith.

This book, then, is about swimming—or, a little more exactly—about journeying in the water, about the world of the swimmer among sandbanks and shoals, through skerries and beneath great cliffs, up fast rivers and slow ones, of the swimmer islanded in the golden evening on some remote mountain loch. We shall need only a big thrusting rubber web on each foot, a mask for the face and a short tube to break every so often into the air.

7

Essentially the swimmer with this simple equipment is free. He is not strapped to metal cylinders or pledged to their fragile throats. Aqualungs are necessary for journeys to great depths, but they are bulbously helpless in windy shallows or among rock-torrents. They have always to be dialled and metered, and the wearer must count and conform to landward minutes. He must never relax; he is land-living air-breathing man with a new tool, steering his environment to strange places. He must return when the clockwork tells him; human, calculated, time presses on his shoulder always. I certainly do not deprecate such diving; it is fascinating, but quite different from the free swimming I am going to describe. It is an exciting, brief and complicated visit, charged with expeditionary pleasures, a technological advance into unknown territory; and so intellectually satisfying that the essential preliminary to aquatic enjoyment as I understand it is lacking—and this essential preliminary is simple animal competence and mental passivity.

Mask, fins and snorkel are merely appendages of the body, making it more adept for the water and not distracting the mind with the nag of terrestrial custom. For in the water all experience is new, or long-since forgotten, and the brain must compile a fresh set of acceptances and rejections. And while you watch the formulation of this new code by the animal faculties, its learning and its automatic application, then you begin to comprehend your double vision, and enter a world more clearly integrated with space and time.

For space has been freed from the bias of gravity and become truly three-dimensional; in this new space every gesture evokes movement and every sensation records it, and your muscles revel in the sudden exchange. Space also appears intellectually more meaningful, converging on you now from immensities beneath as well as from above. And the fourth dimension no longer escapes, dispersing to its own twin infinities. In the water, we are above Time. We watch it rotating far below, in the slow accumulation of continents, in the scuttling sea-bed generations; as we float at the surface, looking down from the still axis, we can grasp it from outside, could bring it up beside us no more than a fistful of mud and shellfish.

When one is easy in the water, therefore, discordances irritating mind and body dissolve away, and a curious exaltation takes their place. As far as I can judge, all such swimmers have experienced this exaltation, though their account of it reflects their own way of life. It can be likened to the effect of great mountains, or music or verse, or religious revelation, or what have you; but all who have encountered it have gone to the brink of some unusual understanding, known a shiver of eternity.

One may simply indulge such thrills, as some have paraded their sensibilities around the music of Palestrina or the pinnacles of the Mer de Glace, until the stimulus of novelty has faded and only the memory, coming sudden as at the cry of a seagull, provokes a nostalgic, spinal, echo; or one may attempt to explore these sensations further, moving—carefully, for their balance is delicate—beyond them and thereby come no doubt upon rewards.

However we seek to explain our fascination in the water, it exists. Let us leave the matter there, meantime. And as this book is largely concerned with the personal experiences of a free-swimming human being (it is not, I repeat, a text-book or a guide) perhaps I should first describe how I came to explore the water at all, and why I did so.

# 2
## *About beginning*

REACH, and one and two and R E A C H, and one and two
and R E A C H, and one ... The voice vanishes upward, water
peals inward; choking, coughing, toes scraping the tile edges,
a small boy staggers upright. Very good, that was THREE
whole strokes on your own. Spit into the gutter, now. Try
again. Come forward. REACH....

No more difficult, one supposes now, than learning to walk;
yet the swimming lessons came late. I had already been able
to walk for some seven or eight years before I was, twice
each week, handed over for an afternoon's half hour to Mrs
Veale. She lives on still, large and putty-fleshed, white-beckon-
ing, clad in wet black wool, disembodied in the splash and
clangour of every swimming pool. And every swimming pool
presents the same sensations—the smack-smacking of bare feet
behind the swing doors, the creak of the iron turnstile, damp
smell of towels, and the red-faced, fuzz-headed procession
passing out as you enter clutching your hard new ticket; then
inside those doors, the great pale green shivering jelly squared
by its wet pavement, the tang of chlorine, the dank little
cubicles with water on the seat and with one bent and insufficient hook for coat and jacket and tie and shirt and
trousers and pants and vest and socks, and whose cold sisal
mat, like a sea animal, noses your freshly peeled feet.

Hoots and echoing water-smacks and bounce-board leaps
from the proficient, but you are led, toe-cringing, to Mrs
Veale. She stands in the shallow end, receiving, face white
and faceless now beneath a tight white rubber cap, pock-
marked, in a black woollen costume dry above but sagging at
the wet edges, her limbs a dead plastic white against the green
jumping water. You take to the cork-soled steps. The cold
seep rises, succeeded by tepid anaesthesia. Toes bottom on

sharp slippery tiles. Walk to Mrs Veale. Deeper, now. Above, ah, the belly; fingering the chest. Almost buoyant, you rise breathlessly on toes. Now ... BEND forward and REACH.

And you were launched on to the excited water that was licking and slapping your face, your legs puzzling their own drill out behind, one toe, furthest out, hopeful on a sloping tile, arms REACHING out to Mrs Veale who advanced slowly and ritually backward, intoning her crook-fingered benediction, and your straining eyes followed the veins printed on her white rubber thighs as you reached, and reached, and reached again.

Then there were intervals with strange wheeled machinery from which you dangled in rough webbing, and you were let down on to and into the surface, while you fought to remember the curiously perverse movements of the breast stroke; and you fought faster and faster as the rope slackened. Weeks passed, months, ears filled with water and receding incitations. And, finally, when you had threshed back far enough from your seven or eight years of land-scrambling, the strain vanished and the round gutter at the other side bobbed rapidly nearer and could be grasped with as easy a rhythm as the stretch and breast-launching that had brought you there.

He can swim.

So the journey to the Deep End began, convoyed by the powerful black woollen cruiser while lesser craft whistled and ducked—or were pushed—aside; you felt the untouchable bottom dropping away from beneath you, and the leaping surface became calm and relaxed. The anxieties of take-off were over. You gained depth over deeper green, almost blue, water, luxuriously velvet and satisfying, especially beneath the dripping shadow of the springboard, so long a symbol of inaccessibility. A gulp of momentary chlorine, a clutch at the handrail; but the gods did not scold, and the cruise continued.

And after this, why recount the other explorations of the cage? I could nose from side to side and from end to end, savouring the change of surface texture and the tactile excitement of steps encountered, predictably, at each corner. I learnt, unaided, side and back strokes and (encouraged by the blue-veined Mrs Veale) stretched myself out on the lapping counterpane, head backward and belly up, and so floated, hung by a breathless thread.

This way master of two dimensions, I tried the third. Forcing entry from above was easy. A shallow jumping-in broke itself sharply, padded in splashes. A deeper one produced a momentary greenish bubbling down, a squat on the tiles, a thrust, and a similar rocketing up; and a great burst through the surface proclaimed victory. But scarcely a victory over the depths; so brief a visit merely emphasized how bound I was to the surface. I tried quietly in corners, submerging my head, straining not to breathe. Ears plugged themselves and hair floated off. I opened eyes very slowly. But there was only a vague green glow, followed instantly by a sharp red pain, and for minutes afterwards I tried to rub away the chlorine and the eyelashes. However often I tried, I remained blind beneath the water. At home I made more attempts, head in washbowl and teetering on a balanced stool: again the eyefuls of hair.

Despairing, I asked others. Did they see? Oh, yes, they saw. What did they see? Oh, people: legs and arms. And what did they look like? Oh, arms and legs; and bubbles. But surely it was more interesting than that, and I was shut out from this mysterious world while the unseeing gazed their empty fill.

Eventually, I could glaze open just enough to retrieve the customary comb on the bottom, but only when I had got down there and squatted on top of it; the glaucous fuzz, rounded to opacity at a yard, crystallized my impotence. However, these attempts did accustom me to being below the surface—but not to swim there, for with this blindness I had to move cautiously in case I knocked my head against the tiles or wandered beneath some hurtling high-diver; an eyeless toad, I probed about the bottom of the big green jar.

Being now licensed as Able to Swim, I was allowed to venture on the margins of the great sea. There I remember vividly rides on the tied-together inner tubes of motor tyres, taken in the laced brown froth of various sandy beaches.

Clutching and astraddle, I would push myself out towards the retreating throat of the last wave, feet riddled by the travelling grains, and when the next blow had been gathered and sent at me, I broke it with a juddering prow and sailed forward over more acquiescent depths, looking back as the lurcher reeled on against the shore. Occasionally there was an upset; but I never saw beneath—eyes tight, sand-spitting, I struggled up at once. Nor was I ever out of my depth, or far from land; mysterious currents were said to lurk on that shallow unfathomable coast.

But they were exciting, these visits to the sea-line, strange extensions of a land life. The airborne unbodied head enjoyed its new position inches above a mile's horizon, limbs frisked irresponsibly below. The fresh smack and pummel of the waves, the cool blast of wind, the mountains rising behind hours of sun-wet sand, were stimulating deviations from grass and leaves, earth and dusty stones.

Growing older, I became a fairly strong swimmer, able to progress for as long as the water felt warm. I used a varied repertoire of strokes, and changing them about compensated me a little for being deprived of the wonders no doubt unrolling beneath. I found pleasure in the different speed and water-pattern of each stroke; to have used only one was as unthinkable as spending a three-hour dance repeating the waltz step. Though able to thresh along in an inelegant breathless crawl, I never enjoyed that stroke, and never persevered with it. Doubtless this was due to my own limitations, but that furious speed seemed only an end in itself and, even in the most expert, appeared to be accompanied by extravagant expenditure of energy; the pounding and shouldering compared so unfavourably with the effortless quiet of the true water animals. It was in fact undignified, like the plunging of a racehorse forced across a river. Also, I could never see a thing during the crawl, and hurtling on with clenched eyes was as disagreeable to well-developed preservative instincts as schüssing on skis in the dark, or jumping the last six feet of an unfamiliar descent; one never knew....

Apparently a man may be of positive, negative or neutral

buoyancy. To discover his category he must go out of his depth. He must tread water. Then he must stop treading water and let out his breath. If his nose remains above the surface, he is positively buoyant. If he sinks then, but can remain above the surface when his lungs contain air, he is of neutral buoyancy. If, his lungs crammed full of air, he still, most disconcertingly, sinks, then he is negatively buoyant and had much better remain with solid earth beneath his feet and the thin air around him. I have found this classification useful, and it may explain why many fast and powerful swimmers become rapidly exhausted on a trip of medium length—say, of two or three hours or so. One friend of mine has to fight merely to stay afloat, and conversation with him is impossible in the water. However, leaden bones need not disqualify you nowadays from long aquatic journeys; but more of that later.

I discovered my own positive buoyancy by a more rigorous test. When at school I had taken to swimming in the river as a change from rowing on it. That wide deep water, alder-edged and fly-haunted, had a smooth black silk surface exquisite to press apart; and there was always, a few inches above the surface and beneath which it was pleasantly ceremonial to move, a dancing canopy of gnats, golden in the evening. One's progress was agreeably measured and applauded by the numberless sanded bays and indentations among the leaning alders, and by the occasional ebony snags and stumps, whose acknowledgements one sidled carefully past.

One evening I was stroking slowly up a lonely stretch of this river after a hard afternoon's sculling. Obviously, I had done too much exercise that day, for one leg began to develop a stabbing, and then a continuous, pain. It contracted uncontrollably. Presumably this was cramp. I had considered cramp before, though never experienced it. So I turned to one of my twin insurances, the river banks. Inevitably, I was slow. Inevitably, also, the other leg developed the same symptoms. So, as if I rode a collapsing rubber tube, I paddled on with both arms. One of these became paralysed as well. At this crisis, fortunately, animal sense took over and instead of fighting towards the bank I went with the current, flicking inwards with one good arm and a spasmodic hand, until I beached in a grass-grown sandy bay. Even after vigorous massage, it was nearly dark before I could limp back along the bank towards the boat. I remember thinking how curious it was that I had been able to direct myself in the water but quite unable even to support my weight on land. There was of course no time for fear in the water and it had no chance of developing when I was once ashore; for added to a survivor's usual euphoria was the exaltation of the elect. It was something to be positively buoyant.

In more sober retrospect this incident made clear how poorly fitted is the human physique for even simple surface swimming. So much effort is wasted even in the easiest stroke most faultlessly executed. And what use are short sausage feet in the writhe and roar of those enticing rapids? Never could they kick you easily, rapturously clear, as the salmon leaps, or the twisting otter. Never could they serve a desire to penetrate, to become saturated with, the turmoil and the black secrecy of that long-abandoned element. So I remained land-bound, occasionally water-visiting; but blind below and tethered above.

This world of water, where every movement of limbs was a delight, what must it contain? Even mere cruising on its surface, among truncated rocks and the small liquidity of wave-lets, off the calm shore on a summer evening, was so reward-ing; and if rewarding in this ridiculously constricted head-gaping, eyes-fixed pose and with limbs slipping wastefully through its elusiveness, how much more satisfying if eye and body were tuned to follow it exactly, precisely responsive to all its flicker of moods, free as this golden light that rippled across its surface and vanished so tantalizingly into the depths.

Much later, the permission came. Permission to enter the water as a water animal.

After the many rumours, at last they were available, those curious flippers that strapped to one's feet and that had been copied so dramatically from the Polynesians by the frogmen of the recently ended war. I bought a pair—which I still have —of a large, heavy, fairly flexible American design. They had an appetizing smell of fresh, virgin rubber. They looked functional and competent. I flapped them hungrily in the air, swirled the washbowl with them in anticipation.

The next day I tried them in the river—a fast river this time, possessing a clear stretch between two linns and being split there by a long wooded island. My friend, a strong swimmer and without fins, slipped off across to the island. I pulled on these heavy rubber pads and, feeling rather ridiculous, platted down the stones to the river's edge. In any depth at all, I could not walk forwards; the great web caught the water and pushed my foot back. So I minced in backwards. Obviously, you should put these things on once you are well in the water. I had chosen a small bay for entry so that I could launch out and try a few strokes before meeting the fast main stream. I flung out on my back and threshed in a slow, loose-kneed kick that took over naturally.

I kicked, and the water answered at last! I was a cyclist whose slipping chain had suddenly caught the sprocket, and thighs leapt to the challenge. Harder, and I drove right out into the current. It bore me sideways, but a twist and steady, luxurious threshing took me up into it again, and within a few more strokes my back ridged and bundled on to the pebbles of the island.

As I sat there gazing at the swift weaver-work of river water chasing and ringleting past, and at the grotesque, absurd, frog feet sticking up out of it, eddies gurgling round them, I realized that here at last was the answer. The years ahead opened to opportunity. A procession of rivers jostled to lakes; lakes flowed together, shouldered aside islands and emptied to the sea; waves carried me onward, strange beaches beckoned. All—rivers, lakes, exotic oceans—all were mine. I was out of the prison at last!

Exalted, I raced my companion back; I was ashore when he was still in midstream. I lent him the fins; he foamed away, while I hobbled after, ghost limbs flailing a vacuum.

Fins on again, I journeyed upstream towards the linn. Lying

back, I watched the rise and fall of muscles and the curdling satisfaction of the wake. Perceptibly, every movement of a leg drove the river banks past me; every relaxation of effort and the banks slowed, the river gathered up beneath me and then, the banks reversing, I was moving off downstream and my head coming round. Then again, one kick and the river relaxed a little, more kicks and the banks recovered themselves and set off obediently downstream once more. Bending knees and twisting, I swung round to gaze upstream at the linn, its rinse creaming over a rocky shelf into mixed water beneath. But I kept well away. I could not see below, clear though the water was at the shallow edges; I knew nothing of any possible currents; besides, my ankle straps had not been sufficiently tested—suppose they were to come off here! I had no reactions ready; I was newly born into an unknown more than half of the world. So I swung back again downstream.

I tried the crawl, but it seemed pointless to bury my head in a moiling bow wave when all the glorious day spun round me—green of crag-hung birches, wet sprays of fern, the rich peat-and-cream river and the white sailing clouds in a blue sky; and surely these leg strokes gave power and satisfaction enough. So for a long time I dallied and circled, or tunnelled up river with furious energy, to cease, and drift, circling, down once more; while my friend sat on the bank and ate the sandwiches.

With fins, then, I was at last a water animal; or—a water animal again? For this seemed the only element I had known, sensitive and understanding; unlike the clumsy earth, either so staggeringly absent or so solidly there. But I was still blind, with no more than a surface liberty.

I had, however, applied at the same shop for vision.

A mask, therefore, and a snorkel tube followed. I practised with them in the familiar strangulation of a wash-basin. My previous blindness had only partially been due to unwieldy eyelashes; human eyes in water are all poor sighted. Because of the different refractive properties of air and water, light entering the eye directly from water is focused off the retina,

17

giving a blurred image. With a mask, air intervenes and the image is focused correctly.

The mask was all that it promised, once hair had been winkled out from its grip so that water no longer wept down into my eyes. I saw, as through mescaline, the white rubber plug, the curiously significant brown spotted chromium chain that held it, and the tiny labyrinth of cracks marbled on the enamel glaze. Even in this unpretentious microcosm a new vision was preparing itself. The snorkel was more difficult; I found the rubber tooth-grip awkward—even now I bite it unconventionally—and the celluloid ball caged at the top closed my escape hatch. I removed ball and cage and breathed more easily; myself and the water would argue without any doubtful mediation.

All, then, was ready for the trial. The sea awaited me, a mile or so away. I would go and look beneath it, peer under the fringe of those millions of tons, teeming and boundless. The unknown two thirds of the globe began at the end of the next road.

# 3
## *About sandy shores*

This first sea had a sandy shore: several miles of pale curving coast, dune-backed, and, that day, a rather greyish water somewhat ruffled but subdued and with only glassy colourless wavelets running about on the wet sand.

I waded in, clutching the unfamiliar equipment. I pulled on the fins when water reached waist level, performing a gasping pirouette, nervous lest I dropped them. Then I washed the mask, spat on the glass as instructed, washed it again and squeezed it on. I jammed the uncompromising snorkel mouthpiece between my teeth. Breath blew and echoed down the tube; wind whistled across its unsteady end. I felt unfocused and ridiculous, could see very little, and lumbered embarrassedly out into deeper water. Headbands bit painfully, and my distant body appeared to be cold. Sand, stirred up by wading, ground in somewhere between toes and rubber. Neither of sea nor of land and jostled by both, I was miserable.

Deeper in, chin on the jittering water, I blinked; sunlight jerked off the wavelets, dazzling the glass. It was time to begin. I bent my head and my legs floated. I kicked myself horizontal, face down, tube up; and looked.

After the cold submergence of the head, the dancing of light stopped, the sun and air vanished, and the green embrace took over. I breathed calmly and easily, in green suspension. The sand beneath was pale green and swayed gently. There was no sound, nor conscious absence of sound; sound had no meaning here. All the senses were turned to light, and to the infinitely gentle stroking of the water on the body. Sight was limited, green and cloudy and focused on the few dancing upper grains of the vast floor stretching beneath; sensation of the current, of the colder and warmer drifts, enwrapped the body and rounded its awareness, passing over its

19

small awakened hairs, so that it became a light and sensitive thing fingering the drift of tide. How one became for the first time aware of the whole body—with its weightlessness and its warm potential of action in this receptive greeness, with its dependence on the harsh bright air above and yet with its curious deep aquatic satisfaction!

I had been fortunate to make this beginning off a sandy shore. For the visual distractions in these places are fewest. All I saw was green water-light and green-gold sand, and the curves of the sand ripples echoed the slowly rippling light— or water, for light here is one with water, the upper water brightening to silvery green, the lower water to the deeper sea-blood, the colours and the medium being the light itself; with no more suggestion of a single external sun than there is among the traceried radiance of Chartres nave.

Along such sandy coasts the senses can feed on the pure medium itself, with eyes and limbs; for the limbs are—indeed the whole body is—linked in one exquisite organ of sense. One flick of a finger swivels the world round the curious gaze.

I found that I could not sink, in any position. I could hang like a mosquito pupa from the surface, tube poking through and knees drawn up and clasped in folded arms. I rose and fell with the waves, warm and comfortable. There was no physical apprehension, no fear of sudden extinction from cramp; at least I would take a long time to drown and surely could think something up in that period.

But I must try and dive. I will not detail the timid duckings and dabblings. Let me describe the first competent dive I made there. Floating on my belly, I breathed in deeply, exten- ded arms, and bent down. Perhaps my legs rose cleanly out of the water, perhaps they did not. All I knew was a sudden effortless propulsion of the sand up towards me. I raised my head a little and the rest of the body followed, cruising along just above the sand, the ripples contoured on its surface undulating as they passed below like small hills beneath a glider, their grains and small stones framed hypnotically in succession before my eyes.

When I grabbed the sand to stop, my fingers melted away

and I rose. Down-kicking, I plunged back deeper, clutched whole armfuls of sand to my chest and lay there, gazing about me. On all sides pale sand petered into formless green. After how far? I had no standard for distances but it would seem thirty or so feet. Above, some ten feet above, a flickering silver ceiling dimpled its patterns. This surface was a defined upper membrane, a true frontier.

My blood complained, so I rose, flicked easily, and burst through. Immediate raging light, coarse texture and crude colour; and welcome air. Floating, and with the surface limned across the mask, I compared both halves of the world in a voluptuous mastery of observation. Bisected, I became detached. Already I was dehumanized, and the hypnosis of this flickering division easily stilled the animal. For a rapid dissolution into Nirvana this two-phase contemplation may be strongly recommended; even the most impure can readily take a trip along its twinned and separate disappearances.

But I had little thought just then for the beatific vision; I was too much concerned with learning to live below water. Down there, I discovered I had no fear of suffocation. With so much to see and explore, there was not time to think about breath-holding; to cease breathing came naturally, and so did the signal to return for more air. Just as rock-climbing allows no opportunity for fright or vertigo, there being too much to do—too many, or too few, holds to plot for—so in this diving I was far too alert and receptive to the outer world to bother about indulging a beleaguered self.

Nor was that outer world terrifying. Any strangeness, any physical unfamiliarity, lay only in the absence of breathing and of sound. Both these deprivations were incurred auto-matically and appeared equally trivial—the new importance granted to vision and movement drove them out of mind. Reassured by the eyes, limbs were flattered by the confidences of the water; freed from their long burden they were open at last to every memory of their ancient home. Scent and sound could drop away, for the exchange was worth it.

Nor was the loss of gravity strange. It seemed much more reasonable to glide in any position and in any direction without effort; to find the surface above, below or on either side, to see your fins black above you scattering bubbles from the sun, to sweep along on your back watching that silver ribbon unroll farther and farther away behind you until sand brushed your hair; to rise feet first, or sideways, or to hover in any position. The joys of weightlessness could be savoured without infringing outer space.

To revel in instant motion, in motion rewarding every twist and bunching of muscle, in obvious motion seen by eye and felt by skin—this delight was not strange. Rather did it seem strange to have clambered about for so long on legs, stumping a thick earth and beating an uncomprehending air. Yet that air would summon you, tightening its insistence on the heart; so you must go back briefly to pay the dues, and then come down again. To breathe in harmony with this new intimate world one would not plug into an aqualung with its edited cavernous echoes, but rather invite the water itself into the lungs, and allow it out again. Fish have the advantage.

But those are drowning thoughts. There is everything still to explore. So I threshed the surface and moved on, head down, eyes searching the sand, breathing easily through the invisible, unfelt tube. The crawl stroke needed least effort in this position. The breathing roll is unnecessary and of course vision—surface with the head raised, submarine when relaxed —is unobstructed. A good speed is readily kept up. The passage of objects—stones, weed-clumps, patches of sand—on the bottom measures progress. But when floating apparently stationary I could detect a movement of the sea floor, slipping away almost imperceptibly; some current was taking me gently aside. Also—though this was difficult on a purely sandy shore—the direction of these currents and their strength could be judged by the streaming of weeds to one side like trees in a wind, or by the ceaseless bowling along the bottom of small debris away into the darkness, like desert tumbleweed in a storm. These were the signs, and they were hoarded carefully.

Of course, over deeper water, with the bottom no longer visible from the surface and where I stared down into beckoning formless green, there were no signs. Here one's directional sense could be hopelessly wrong. Often, supposedly pounding along parallel to shore, head down and green-dreaming, I looked up into the bright sun to see if I had yet rounded that white sandy point I was making for and found instead the sardonic greeting of an empty horizon; so, then, an abrupt turn. There is, even with good visibility below, no real knowing how the submarine landscape coincides with the subaerial one; there can be fussy underwater obtrusions and retractions quite unrelated to the sweep of coast. Rarely, on this small human-wandering scale, do the two worlds touch other than at the flickering intangible surface.

These sandy undershores stretch on, undulating gold against the green, in small ripples and in vast smooth banks. In shallower places the sun lights clear upon the sand, with a small cloud of grains, disturbed by the overhead swell, dancing on every ridge: pieces of shell, white, blue, grey and black fragments, with thin black shreds of shore-dried weed sucking back and forward along the ranks. Further out, the bed is firmer, less disturbed, and ripples away in greater and lesser ridges and valleys, subsiding to darker green distance. Just above the sea floor drift thin fans of weed, frail paper-white or green, sparse and untidy as litter. A crab may appear, jerking suddenly out of the sand or running sideways fluently across ridges. A disturbance, settling slowly, shows where a dab has leapt up and scurried away. Sometimes you may see one of these flatfish pegged out on the sand, its ridged averted eyes regarding you, before it bunches and flaps off hen-like among clouds of dirt. Nearer shore, in schools of sand-ghosts, black-eyed and invisible, shrimps and prawns flick and scatter, burrow and stare at you, crowding in behind as you pass, like the shades peering at Orpheus. And there are colonies of worms and molluscs, with small feathery feelers or mouths, tubed and fanned, pushed brazenly or hopefully above the sand; as you approach, waves of retraction precede you. Occasionally, through the clear green skies of this desert a white dome trailing ribbons, ridiculously resembling Mrs Caudle's night cap, pulses slowly past; intricate in colour and successive concentric depths, these jellyfish fascinate by their purposeful journeys to or fro some private infinity, attended by their delicate and murderous strings.

But life is scarce here, and delight is in motion, in twisting and coiling within the golden-green box, in the downward sweeps to colder water and the urgency about the ears, to sand rough on the chest; delight in the bubble-decked rise to the surface; or, pausing there, in the gazing again over miles of liquid glittering under the sun; or in dreaming across to the thin, distant shore. Then a breath, and down again to the slow tempo, to subtleties that comb across the skin, to intoxicating glides along and over buried ridges, thrust of water answering thrust of legs. On and on across the fascination of desert, the glass-green plate trembling above for infinite miles.

The surface pleasures of these shores are equal in their immensity. Usually the shore is flat, and at mask-height from half a mile out it is no more than a white and gold rim of one slip of the green horizon, without meaning as land. There exists only the flat, shifting colour around you and the slow cloud procession above; and the focused, burning sun. Or, on cold, grey days, the bare fundamentals of water and arching air, a darker and a lighter grey. The lesser waves that roll you melt into this vastness, and their small slappings and sucks choir into a single soundless voice. Drifting in a boat, one is moved by these things. But out there alone as I have described, with no distractions of carpentry, gunwale or seat, bodyless and drunk into the hugeness of water, how much greater the wonder, how much nearer the imminent dissolution!

Therefore, to break up such transcendentalism, you lie back and kick largely and bestially, sending up great clods of white water, a lusty tower visible for miles across the astonished sea, spattering and raucous, while gulls twist overhead.

These sea-birds may sometimes embarrass the swimmer, especially off exposed sandy coasts. I met trouble from them on my first visits to the wide bays of eastern Scotland. When walking out over the sand and wading the broad shallows I noticed birds dotted in clusters on a spit, and others circling above them; their cries threaded the flat boom of waves. I soon left them behind and thought no more. Later that afternoon, drifting far out on the surface gazing down, I became uncomfortable. My scalp tingled: something had its eye on me. I searched the bottom, and the green surrounds, and saw nothing. The silence deepened. Then a blow of air punched past the snorkel, followed by a remote scream. Jerking my face out of the water, I saw a bird skimming away in front. Looking round, I saw another diving at my head, screaming in rage: wings and legs folded back, beak and eyes sharply aimed—red beak, yellow eyes—and white hurtling body. I waved arms, kicked and splashed and, more relevantly, dodged with my head; but at the last moment the tail came down, one wing flicked and, still shrieking, my attacker peeled off. More were descending, a spiral of Stuka terns bright in the sun. Their furious speed was alarming. But I soon realized that, wisely, they had no intention of striking me: at that velocity their own necks would be snapped by the collision. Perhaps they might risk a glancing slash, but a serious blow could only be accidental. Still, the consequences of an over-confident tern's miscalculation might be dangerous. So I retreated, watching warily and taking care not to dodge into their line of last-minute evasion, which appeared fairly predictable. I swam backwards, eyes fixed on them until, in hoarse triumph, they called off their raids. Ever since then I have kept half a mental ear to the surface, finding that the snorkel tube sensitively records aerial disturbance and that one soon becomes attuned to this unfamiliar source of information.

That episode made clear that I no longer represented the known and feared terrestrial Lord of Beasts, driving aside unfortunate fowls. I was an unprotected, edible, wriggle of meat. I had to allow for more aggressive and much more competent beings in this new environment. I began to look about beneath the surface with unease. I had taken account by now of tides and currents and suchlike physical hazards: or at least I was ready to meet any new physical hazard. Many years among mountains had coaxed, or hammered, out the necessary rational response to that kind of challenge. But to recognize oneself as a pursuable interloper—within a mile of an Angus bus-stop—required a disturbing readjustment.

Having fled so far out from my enemies, I could see no trace of the sea floor. I pulled up legs, plump with red juice, out of the black water and its unseen jaws. But I could scarcely rise above the waves, and therefore it seemed desirable to dive right down and convince myself there were no sharp predators below. On the surface I felt lonely and helpless, one clothes-peg strung on a long line, small but protruding unbearably up and down, visible for miles.

As I dived I took a ball of light with me, but gradually its power dimmed and eardrums began to pluck painfully. The mask contracted on to my face; I blew air down my nose to keep it off. I began to wonder if I was still going down, and not travelling away obliquely on an endless route in mid-water. Then all at once the sea floor rose into view; flat grey mud, with small stone-like concretions and a weed or two. I welcomed it as one welcomes a mountain summit in mist. I knew where I was. Reassured, I touched its slime and drove back upwards through clouds of bubbles, darkness falling away behind.

Bright and birdless was the sky. Well and safely bottomed was the sea. Toothless and empty was mid-water. Yet I paddled shorewards humbly enough, looking around—and above—rather too frequently. I discovered later that this animal prudence—it hardly seemed fear, for curiosity and excitement salt it too appetizingly—this caution would rein me in far more tightly off rockier shores, where boulder and weed and deep-drowned pot-hole were peopled with expect-ant eyes and teeth. But there at least I too had shelter; this long empty underwater desert of a sandy shore sank to the unprotected bone. I avoided the spit off the bay, crowded with terns who disdained to remark my modest and circuitous return.

Coming inshore to the sand is a pleasant experience. It is the most pleasant to drift in, head-foremost, through the warming water. The sand beneath slopes gradually upward. There may be several false shore-lines, shelves that nearly make the surface, where sand-grains jump excitedly. From the shore they would be seen as shallow bars. Your hands pluck you forward over these ridges, spray drenching your hair, grit rubbing your belly, until the sand drops away into colder, quieter water.

At length the final shallows arrive; the waves will then move you in perceptible bursts, their noise and wash muttering or shouting into your ears, pulling at your shoulders. Around you the grains and debris shuttle to and fro, ahead the wavelets explode. You nose onward, greedy for the last half-inch of clear warm water (oh, how warm is this small shore-water after the cold maturity far out)—and then you lie aground as the wave retreats, blinking in the sun. You prepare to rise on your arms, gather your strange muscles, when the next wave collects your feet and bundles you forward; again you are rinsed free, grains burrowing into fins and hair. Enough, you stagger upright, raise the mask and flap the last few yards. But even with fins pulled off, how clumsy you are! Prolonged swimming upsets, for many minutes, your land-built uprighting reflexes. You sway, often collapse. The horizon rotates, or slants giddily. And how painful, slow, how ludicrously contrived is the progress you make by pushing one leg out, learning to balance on it, then dragging through and swinging the other prop out before that one; and repeating the whole weary business, with separate clenching and unclenching of desperately-remembered muscles; while the rest of the body, able to do nothing, sits heavily above, a bewildered spectator, helpless as a jellyfish cast on the shore. The progress of Molloy.

So to collapse on the dunes, a punctured sea animal dusty with unfamiliar soil, among shrill turf in the bright sun. And it is then you begin to feel cold. Fingers, arms, shake uncontrollably. You are suffering back into your flesh, into the world you were born for.

B

# 4

## *About stony and rocky shores*

Let us pass along the coast to places where sand gives way to gravel, where banked hoards of pebbles take over and boulders are planted, large and heavy, and the basal rock itself stirs up and moves out into the sea.

Water is darker off a stony beach than off sand. Fingers of sand appearing among underwater pebble-fields beckon brightly from a distance and fish flick darkly across them. Perhaps the most colourful stony bottoms are those of the western sea lochs, where pebbles of every hue glow and dazzle in the sun; provided that the tides rinse them, for in backwaters and brackish reaches a sombre tilth accumulates and the bottle-brown gloom is of apothecaries' cellars—but more of that when we come to the freshwater places. Washed by tides, the mosaic is bright and vigorous; pebbles and boulders in the Torridonian sea lochs, for example, are a polished brick-red—brilliant at noon among intricate white quartzite and in the evening warm with their stored sun beyond the black forests of weed.

In these stony places we meet for the first time the plants. There are sandy bays underwater, broken here and there by patches of stones and boulders, and on these stones the sea-weed bushes are anchored, their hair drawn out and fingered by the tide.

It is warm among the weed, and the tendrils brush silkily upon the skin. In quieter places the clumps rise tall, six feet or more, golden and jewelled with bubbles. They people the flat surface of white sand, flare like sentinels from boulders, jostle in spinneys and copses, and align themselves in vanishing hedges. Among them small fish swim, sun glinting bronze and silver from their backs. These cypress fronds gather into one thick stem planted about its stone with rubbery paws.

28

Pulling downwards by the fronds one can sometimes lift the stone, to exploding crustacean panic, or one can probe and part the tresses, gazing into the red-lichened and mysterious interior.

It is impossible, when threading through these silent illuminated spires, gazing on their richest greens and reds and every shade of luminous gold and olive, diamonded by sunlight, to associate them with the mud-brown wrecks left flat on stones and sand when the tide is out: those flatulent heaps so treacherous beneath your feet. It is a daily wonder, this death and resurrection of the miraculous labyrinth. And exquisite is the pleasure, after stumbling over the collapsed ranks, to ease oneself out into rising water where the sun is switched down into shafts and patches, and watch the assemblages asserting themselves again, luxurious in wine-smooth liveries. The tallest wracks, wristed and knuckled, thrusting towards and sometimes lying along the surface, are starred and tuffeted with soft puffs of scarlet and green, these in turn encrusted with ivory worm-work and small bright coral-like meanderings. Where boulders give way to rocky shelves, there are hanging forests of wrack, enwrapping and slapping rhythmically the barnacled crags, their fronds blown with air-spray from the upper waves.

But so rich is this world, it is difficult to know where to begin a description. On the way into water you may dip your head into a rock pool. Shallowness and blinding light give these miniature landscapes great clarity and chromatic drama; brilliant green scrub dots coralline scarps, wisps of scarlet wink down a twisting white valley: but all is essentially unsatisfying because you yourself are not involved, merely gazing at an agreeably contrived aquarium.

Once immersed, however, you are included. Even in the shallowest water, you see for the first time the full skinless depth of a seaweed frond, lit often as not from within—for the light may join it from any direction. On its unflawed surface painted periwinkles are gliding, their horns searching continually, their shells twisting first one way, then the other. All is in harmony: texture of weed-flesh and snail-flesh, the sliding light and the effortless progression. Your own skin or your rubber glows equally, your own movements flow in the same way. The fish wind, insinuate themselves, in this manner and so the spined crab leaps—to remain poised before floating gently downward, a Nijinsky of the passing ballet. Your ears when they hear, hear the slow roll of waves beyond the reef; and the wind breathes quietly over the snorkel tube.

In places like these there is little desire to examine analytically, to pinch up and catalogue the plants and fish. You have an animal's, and a child's eye. I make comparisons here, I may write that such a clump of weed was like a great swamp cypress hung with moss, birds bright round its turrets: and this picture smacks of that 'terrestrial editing' I foreswore—but how else can I convey, however crudely, the impression? I saw no cypress, neither did such a likeness bother me then; these occasions need no similes. My eyes and my body were aware of a vast lobular fruiting of the sea, towering gold and sunset-brown through the green water, rising from blue anchorage to a silver mirror, complete and satisfying in itself.

So however refreshing this dismissal of language, this irrelevance of human experience, may be below water it cripples any retrospective description. Words lie land-stamped and unsympathetic; aquatic rhythms coil despairingly on a dry page. Aridity or contortion is too often the result.

But let us, despite these hazards of communication, continue splashing to sea among flat-wrack shrubberies, weaving through tall plantations of bladder-wrack, and launch out farther and deeper to where all rocks disappear into the pale sea bed. There is no fear of entanglement with stems on the journey, if movements are unhurried. One must sidle through pawing multitudes, skirt the heavily strung cordage in deeper places. Any hook-up of mask or fins is instantly felt as a gentle pluck, and an equally gentle evasion or retraction removes the hindrance. Only jerks and grabs are dangerous, but they are panic reactions foreign to the rhythms down here and never thought of; still, I always carry a sharp saw-toothed knife, and pat its cork handle for reassurance in pressing, viscous, places.

Push, then, clear of the last shore-weeds and lunge out over hanging cliffs as in one of those space-happy dreams, spiralling slowly down on an invisible abseil to the distant gleam of sand. Below you the sun lies wrapped among deep-water laminarian forests. These memorable groves are at their finest off the West Highland coast. Ten to twenty feet high, with thigh-thick stems and yards-long straps for leaves, they line the threshold of the depths. From above they resemble the undulating canopy of a tropical rain-forest, spangled with lit clearings. Beneath them lies the most delectable of waterscapes.

As you sink lower the green haze clears and brightens. Details are sharp again, colours scintillate. Trunked, elephant-browed and hung with elephant ears, caparisoned in gold and purple, the laminarians below you shuffle aside to make way for the rising patches of white sand. Small fish flit above them; below, among the jungled trunks, browse heavy velvet wrasse.

With great effort, for it is thirty feet down, you urge yourself beneath their palm-lobes, breast the sand and, turning, wrap arms around a rubber bole. Then all exertion ceases. The vast weight of water above weighs down in satisfaction. About you, fish proceed on business from the ends of globe and time, picking up and spitting out, moving on. Light trickles through leaning fronds above you, stretches on the textured sand beside you. Glade after glade repeats, echoes into infinite distance: a shuddering hypnosis. Eyes are uncoupled, your brain washed, by the invading salt. The hooded groups regard you gravely, like druids of inestimable age. The enchanted forest closes in, and it takes great resolution to drive out the brine, seize again your own bauble of time, unclasp and rise from this primeval floor, to kick up and wriggle free, tunnel out to the contemporary coughing air.

Then you float, gasping in great draughts of open sky, milk-blue horizon and lean black headlands. Far off a lobster boat sputters, bow smacking the waves in odd, irregular rhythm.

As the tide falls, these laminarian forests rise nearer to the air and the narrowing water between swaying frond and surface thickens with small feeding fish. One may move through their incurious crowds towards an emerging rock, yellow and barnacled; round it—for this is a neap tide—disconsolate humps of laminarians are being exposed. To drag oneself through resistant gelatinous branchwork on to sharp mineral is a refreshing change, and it is pleasant just to lie there, half-lapped by sea and air, observing the identity of frond and rubber, limb and stem, your own relaxation harmonizing with the floating weed and with the gentle submersion of an indolent shoreline.

The waters may be lazy then, but in a rising wind their muscles tauten. You slip off the rock with the lifting swell, wriggle through agitated weed and bore out some distance before turning to look at the coast under these new conditions. White breakers hit the rocks and under water you dimly see air-falls, cataracts of air pulsing down each gully, hanging, then vanishing upwards again. Hurricanes and air-blizzards work and wrench among the weed, scavenge the basins. Fish and crabs crouch there, air-drenched, limpets grip against the blast; the unskilled do not survive long. Far out and safe, clinging to a rock on the pitching sea bed you see waves mirrored inversely above you, breaking on great shore-peaks like thunderclouds, and streams of airspray white as snow-plumes foam off the disappearing summits.

You must pick entrance to land carefully then, for heads and rubber suits are damaged by an unexpected hoist across barnacles, and in high waves safe entry can only be made by accurate riding into sandy gullets, hands well forward, arms raised for protection. With no easy grounding available, a foot-first approach is needed; you back out the fiercest waves and ride in on a chosen green surge till feet hit rock, then bunch forward into a kind of clutching jump, folding yourself on to a picked hand-hold—you must not miss and roll back into the counter-suck, nor become jammed into a crevice. But you should not be caught out like this on an unknown coast in severe weather; the warning signs are obvious enough.

Farther out, surface roughness does not much affect the depths and rarely does one see whole deep-water forests churning slowly to and fro, curdled debris blowing round roots and crowns; the water is usually too murky anyway, even from small breakers, and it is better to hunt above with the white horses. Free of skerries and with a sheltered landing to make for, rough water on the surface is wonderfully exhilarating, especially when the boat is your own unsinkable self. Cork-like you miss the drenches and buffets, and it is surprising how rarely the snorkel is caught in an unexpected wave-crest. Riding and kicking over, between and through the breakers is akin to skiing down a gently undulating gully, movement and wave-scape blending to perfection, but of course there is more relaxation in the water and you have three dimensions at your disposal. Raised on the crest you see the far shore flung beneath you; borne down, downwards, and nothing above you but trampling green feet and perhaps, giddily high beyond the froth, the momentary tip of some remotely anchored mountain peak. I once made such a journey, with wind and tide and a yelping pack of waves, up Loch Torridon from near its rocky constriction on to the safe leeshore of Inveralligin: a memorable afternoon of plunge and slide, and roll-about sun-bathing, framed between the alternate heaves of Beinn Alligin and Beinn Daimh and with occasional flickers of the approaching string of cottages. Homing through the sandy shallows is boisterous and dirty, and the last back-slap that lands you sprawling high on the pebbles is a suitably final gesture from an afternoon of good-fellowship.

But we will describe such times when we come to the chapter on Touring. Here let us continue our first explorations off these rocky coasts, and choose calmer weather, with a playing sun to bring out the colours underwater.

Blossoming beneath are occasional pink chrysanthemums, gay and unexpected pompoms to wink from the sombre laminarian forests. These are sea urchins, vibrant with colour when examined down there, striped purple and pink and white, and clamorous with bright, radiating spears; pluck them and their bristles cringe. But they are best left un-gathered, being porcupines to wet fingers and intolerable to carry far. Left islanded upon a rock until your return, they disappear—stolen by a gull, dislodged by wind, perhaps even shuffling off themselves or, more likely, the rock has been lost among a hundred others or beneath the rising tide. Yet, like flowers, they itch to be picked, for when scrubbed their cool and intricate shell-work traps the dance of sunlight in a bare room, and for years they hold the echoing smell of the sea.

But we must pass on, for we cannot describe the innumerable other sights and hints below, from the flaunted symmetry of starfish—when picked up so disappointingly stiff and horny—to those twitched weed curtains behind which lurk lobsters or worse; but all are immediate excuses for descent and slow rummaging among stones and stem-flesh, all will keep you occupied while the sea in its turn leisurely handles and examines you.

Fish, of course, are the most dramatic objects (apart, perhaps, from seals—but we'll deal with seals later). There are always fish somewhere, exploring like yourself, whiting, pollack, saithe, sea trout, breeds you soon cannot help but recognize at a distance by their posture or turn of fin, as you know a bird by the flick of its tail or a friend by the tilt of his hat. But let us keep them anonymous here, as far as possible; we have not come to capture and label—there is enough of that above—rather to watch and gather understanding of the sea and of ourselves, and to remember again the wonder.

Few sights are more wonderful down here than a shoal of fish, sudden and rapid, startling the eye and most curiously exciting the blood. I was on the bottom one day, in clear water some twenty feet down among fine spacious scenery— sunny glades, weed coppices and occasional rocky divides rising from the white sandy floor. Suddenly, between the tallest rock crest and the surface, flashed a sun-riddled shoal of elvers. Like a great eel itself—twenty feet long, six feet through—this undulating flock passed and repassed above, finally to curl and stream down in a silver rain beside me.

I could hardly disobey. I struck off and joined them, following their aberrations as best I could, stretching to watch their

34

leader—ahead of us all by half a length—and straining to catch his next diversion. The shoal opened out to accommodate me; I could just maintain their pace and for a long half-minute be part of this thrilling organism. All else—rock, weed, surface—disappeared. Ahead, behind and beside me pullulated with shining bodies. Far out in front lay some infinitely receding necessity. But now, for me, air.... Breathless, I struck free, broke surface, gulped and rejoined, cutting across gyres to catch up. Again my neighbours moved aside to let me in. Again the whirling chase through sun and shadow.

Many times since I have done this, and never has the group paid me any attention; when confronted directly, they peel past on either side, their gaze fixed far beyond. To join them and latch on to this obsession, to follow this predestined labyrinth through a blank sea, was to be pulled back through convolutions of brain towards some far white beginning, some distant opening of the tunnel. Certainly it was cathartic—one felt taken apart and rinsed by the ages; and then put together again rather smaller.

I have laid below crags and waited for them to surge from the darkness; have weaved in counterpoint, crossing and inter-crossing, linking their spirals, vanishing with them and appearing again through ravines and cliffs, circusing in great sunlit sandy bowls; and have suddenly felt lost and silent, suspended, and known they have gone; and fear has prickled, bringing thoughts of predators, seals, sharks or killer whales; and just as I would be backing to shelter, like streams of electric bulbs they would pour forth again and all was right with the world once more, on we would dash together.

I had felt the cold draught of isolation; from how many thousands, millions, of years had it come?

Often I have gazed up at swifts darting similarly, rising and falling and sweeping in companies; but on land man is a helpless spectator, clumsy and avoided. His choice has long been made. He takes his dog for a walk.

There are other shoals underwater to meet, but not to join, for they are either too small, or too deliberate and aloof. Tiny

35

clouds of sand-eels and fry flicker in shallows or above a chosen clump of weed; you may pass through them as through a mist of gnats. Or, if you choose to rest and watch them, they approach, fragment to exploratory snuffling individuals about your arms and face, and then at some alarm switch sideways and vanish completely, to re-form many yards away in another busy shimmer. Often sedate groups of larger fish slide into view, each member moving independently of his fellows, each a separate inquisitive being, cocking his separate head, now going a little to one side, now to the other, now lagging quite far behind; but all are bound by a discipline, however flexible, and together they glide away as together they came, the last one speeding to catch up as if drawn by elastic. They are not like the eels, threaded along some ancient necessity. If you approach them, they amble away; if you pursue them, they fly and are gone. You may see them, recovered and decorous, proceeding quietly across the green sand of a neighbouring glade.

Bigger fish, even solitary ones, are few off this particular Ardnamurchan coast I have in mind. Great dark shapes vanish almost as soon as perceived, with a beat and shimmy of tail, and only the clumsier kind can be examined at leisure: richly liveried wrasse snouting the undergrowth, harsh-skinned dogfish shaking irritably from clump to clump, and occasionally, coiled within its selected den, a conger eel. I shall describe later an encounter with this sinister beast and only remark here how its impression of evil emanates from the deliberate hiding of that pallid thigh-thick body, lying there triggered in wait, so that innocent boulders and stones round about also appear tight with fury and itching to spring; and from the clear unwinking intelligence of eyes fed by so alien a light; and of course from the unpleasant immediacy of teeth.

Let us back away. We are too far out from shore and are tiring. Those shivers along the back and behind the shoulders remind us of the hours since the last meal; a flat cold stone lies in the stomach. Darkness is falling back there on the land. The sea's surface is still bright with the low sun, the

36

small gold-fringed waves before us are cheerful enough, but down below distances are gathering together and invading. Already the sea bed is invisible and light has bled out of the shoreward slopes beneath. Another time we will describe the pleasures of nocturnal swimming. This time we must turn on our backs and thresh homewards with a glittering wake, gazing at the red sun and the barred west and at the islands rising out there taller and taller, smouldering and improbable.

Slowly the coldness falls behind, smoother and blacker grows the surface; rock jetties move past to harbour us. Turning to look, we see the head of a quiet inlet approaching, and soon legs are hampered by stems, hands by a warm meshwork; and then shoulders are bumping softly on to the tangle.

There only remains the effort of hauling up and climbing out, the needling of rock on sodden fingers, unbuckling and—strange unlikely mode of progression after such a day among easeful weed-upholstered waters—a lumbering across stones and beach and ditches.

# 5
## About keeping warm and other problems

Now that we have described the first ventures into the sea, from two contrasting kinds of coast, let us dry off a little with a few questions that must have worried any reader who has kept abreast for so long.

Firstly, the perennial enquiry, deprecating and astonished —'But are you not cold? Surely it's all very well in the Red Sea or the Mediterranean, but up here in the north. . . .'

No, I did not feel cold. (Why I use the past tense will become apparent.)

I may have been fortunate in my temperature regulation as I undoubtedly was in the matter of innate buoyancy, but I think not. Entry into a swimming pool was always agony: especially an unheated one. I had never enjoyed bursting straight in, by feet or head. To begin by diving in was notably unpleasant. This did not just stem from natural cowardice or, to put it more kindly, from caution at committing oneself to untested water; familiarity with any particular pool never lessened my dislike of 'immediate total entry'.

Whenever I jumped in straight away, I never seemed to warm up again; much energy had to be expended even to stay reasonably warm, and drifting about brought on severe shivering. I had to leave the water much earlier than if I had entered it slowly in the first place. Slow entry entailed its niggling creep of water-line, and the clinical stages of cooling step by step down the regulation staircase were time-consuming and socially embarrassing; but this purgatory did reward one with much longer enjoyment in the pool—much longer, it was comforting to note, than that afforded to the dashing plungers. Slow entry was of course natural on shallow sandy beaches and one never noticed cold there, splashing in through wind and wave. Neither was chilling evident when mask and fins had to be carried in and fitted on at a dripping half-submergence.

I have discovered a physiological rationale for the benefits of this grudging immersion; I put it forward as a plausible excuse for avoiding a brave and disagreeable plunge. The blood circulating in the body can be thought of as peripheral blood, nearest the skin, and as core blood, deep within the big muscles and vital organs. When bare skin is exposed to cold, the superficial vessels contract so that only a little warm blood traverses these cooled areas, the bulk remaining in the core. If cooling is performed slowly, as by gradual immersion, then the vessels contract ahead of the advancing cold water, and heat loss from the core is minimal. But by the time one is immersed the bulk of the 'peripheral' blood has been withdrawn, still warm, to the core and so does not chill the vital organs. In contrast, a sudden diving entry allows insufficient time for shutting down the circulation of peripheral blood which is therefore rapidly cooled and, when it enters the core, lowers the temperature there. Shivering sets in when the core blood is cooled even slightly, and much energy must be spent to warm this blood up again, energy which would be better employed in allowing the core to tick over at its normal temperature for a longer period.

This explains why the most comfortable entry is made on a cool day; the peripheral vessels are already contracted before you go into the water and little further discomfort is noticed. The worst, as everyone knows, is on a hot sweaty day when the body's cooling mechanism is in full operation, the peripheral vessels being filled with blood from the core; or some time after exercise, with blood still raging below flushed skin. A plunge may be refreshing then, but prolonged immersion is usually not so popular—'Astonishing how cold the water is today . . . and the sun so hot.'

Undoubtedly, also, one does become 'used to it' and I could swim, usually on the move and with little drifting around, for over two hours at a time off the eastern Scottish coast with little inconvenience from cold. A hot meal, and I could return for an hour or so afterwards. That would be in early autumn, after some sea swimming almost every other day from late spring; the first few days finished before the half hour.... On the cold, grey, blustery days of autumn it was delightful to snuggle under the waves as under a counterpane, out of the wind. For once the body is wet, wind cools it more effectively than water does, and on windy days one should avoid standing about in shallows or scrambling over islanded rocks.

After even the best-regulated immersion, one eventually becomes cold. Gradually a tightness is felt in the belly, and draughts tickle the shoulders. You return to land, but even when ashore and possibly numb with chill you may only begin to shiver when you are warming up. Vigorous towelling will bring it on, or exposure to hot sun. You are warming up the periphery; its vessels expand, so that blood entering them from the core loses its heat to the still-cold skin and superficial muscle (your numb arms and legs), and is therefore returned much cooler to the core—which, as your chilliness has warned you, is already near its lower permitted level. Immediately, the shivering reflex starts up, to obtain warmth from muscular contraction.

Sometimes this shivering, though not at all distressing, can be quite crippling. I could never fasten a tie on those days, and buttons vibrated impossibly. Clothes had to be left outside the car, for to try and fit a key to the lock was unthinkable. The best thing for bad shivering is heat applied to the core, as by hot drinks. Externally applied heat excites peripheral circulation before being able to warm the cold subcutaneous mass and so temporarily accelerates core cooling. Alcohol is dangerous if chilling is severe. Though it can be burnt as a fuel deep down, its side-effect is to dilate peripheral vessels (that 'warm glow') and so invite cooling of the core; it certainly provokes ecstatic shivering, if you want that kind of thing. Brandy and malt whisky are for the evening tent—certainly not for half-way waters.

But the unclad swimmer has his warnings, and makes for shore long before his fires are running low. Yet suppose he is delayed? He may be held offshore by interest, or by a stiffer tide than expected. If by interest, then just to bend up the knees and clasp them with the arms, hands in armpits, hanging by snorkel, effectively reduces heat loss. If by a tide, then the greater exertion required speedily warms up the core; of course, fuel for this exertion is very necessary—if meals were a long time before, then glucose sweets (always to be carried somewhere waterproof) should suffice. Yet whatever his precautions the tourer clad only in a swimming costume has but a limited time in northern waters before serious heat loss overtakes him.

A full-length costume is much warmer than trunks. It is especially comforting in those last dives of the day, when the upsweeping embrace of cold deep water about the chest no longer thrills but squeezes out a gasp and leaves its memories back on the surface; you can count your icy ribs. These are times when it is pleasant, and prudent, to sidle among weed crowds, feel their warm breath on thighs and back. Prudent, because after such dalliance no one would go back to the outer water, but gradually levitate to ever shallower, warmer delights and so finish up, of course, on the beach.

Better insulation still is provided by a combination of trunks and a close-fitting woollen jersey. I never went to the extreme of long woollen drawers, for they could scarcely restrict cold water flow over the skin during vigorous leg movements and anyway would become tedious with their flapping; short pants might be more suitable. Jerseys proved comforting, especially to the neck, where much heat is lost, and they allowed arms to remain inactive during leisurely surface cruising; movement of arms, otherwise necessary to prevent muscles chilling, greatly disturbs underwater life. Wet wool exposed to wind remains wet and its constant evaporation cools you long after bare skin would have dried to reasonable warmth; jerseys should be discarded on emergence.

Rough seas and rivers of course provide warmth by friction, but you have to make good the heat lost by this rapid water flow, so that even with jerseys any unprovisioned journey must be relatively short. In practice neither my wife nor I found difficulty in staying three or four hours in the water, provided we had a feeding break. A suitable meal would include a hot drink and plenty of carbohydrate—bread and jam, for example—the most readily utilizable form of fuel. At night one could stoke up with meat and fat. Fat on the person, under the skin, is often claimed of great value in insulation. If this is so, the layers need not be thick, for my wife possesses feminine cushioning in the usual places whereas I may flatteringly be described as lean, and yet I suffered much less from cold water than she did.

You will note that I have been extolling my hardihood in the past tense. This is because I rarely go to water nowadays except in a close-fitting suit of expanded neoprene. As will be recounted later, I was driven to this concession by the freezing agonies inseparable from underwater photography. Once one tastes this rubbery bliss, there is no going back—in northern latitudes, at least—and jeers and recriminations of disenchanted young, who must learn the hard way, have failed to disturb a well-established decadence.

One gains and loses by wearing such a wet-suit. The greatest loss is of that sensitivity described earlier, whereby every hair of the body tells the eddies, and depths and currents record their waves of cooling; you miss the warm brush of weed, and the thrill of thigh-entangled bubbles when you drive down. To set against such a loss is the gain in detachment as you slowly sink, drugged in blubber. Easier than ever, under this narcosis, to lose all surface intricacies, to let them disperse among the bones of continents: to enjoy, undistracted, their infinite dilution. As well as such a spiritual purging, neoprene suits provide you with a fucoid integument blending perfectly with the native sea-flesh around you.

You are no longer pale and conspicuous; relaxation is complete. Hauled out for an occasional air-bathe on some isolated skerry, your limbs rise and fall weightlessly with the sea-swell, impervious to wind or water, warm and without sensation, losing themselves among the floating kelp, being lifted back with it bright into the sun; or, lying higher across the barnacled rock, they dry to the quiescence of exposed bladder-wrack or sea-anenome, dully awaiting the next tide.

But of course the main thing is that these suits are warm. You have a vastly increased safety margin in cold waters. When fit and properly fed you find a six- or seven-hour touring day, with intermittent haul-outs for nourishment and basking, no more tiring than a leisurely hill-walk of the same duration. And you are weather-proof. You may bask in sun or shower, and winds do not exist, nor damp seats. Or at least you do not notice seats as damp. You yourself are always warmly wet.

For naturally the principle of a wet-suit is that you do not remain dry within it. It is not water-tight, but nearly so and the water that does make its way between your own skin and the thick rubbery one seeps in slowly, and out slowly. As expanded neoprene is so excellent an insulator, little of your heat is lost to the outside and the trapped water, usually a mere film, rapidly reaches and remains at bodily heat. You live, therefore, jacketed in warm water or rather water which, being at your own temperature, appears neither hot nor cold and is never noticed. Only violent movements of limbs, especially arms, can drive the old warm water out and let in cold new draughts, but as such exertion raises your temperature, comfort is rapidly restored.

Pulling on and dragging off this skin is tiresome, but the newer suits with an inner nylon lining lack the vacuum-like suck and grip of those made wholly of neoprene. I remember well my first struggles. All clothes were removed. An incautious probe with a sweaty leg resulted in complete adhesion while still below the knee, and in desperate contortions before the rubbery gullet was forced to disgorge the limb. I therefore poured talc into the breeches and rubbed it over my body. Provided I was quick, both legs could be wriggled through and feet, the most quarrelsome parts, shaken out at the ends. Then a massive haul-up below the waist cleared buttocks, and all that remained to do, coughing among the dust clouds, was a smoothing and preening to remove the creases. With nylon linings, these breeches give little more trouble than tight ski trousers, provided the skin is first powdered. Jackets are much easier, though buckling the tail between your legs and zipping up a protesting chest requires practice, and is daunting to chilled hands. Then there are sock extensions for the feet, surprisingly simple. A hood, very difficult to put on, is only required for long trips and I never found gloves necessary except in winter or early spring.

I first wore such a suit on an autumn evening. I stepped out of the house into the dusk, and picked my way through a birch wood to a near-by river—little more than a hill burn —whose water was certainly too cold at that season for the limited swimming its boulder-peppered pools could afford. Branches and grass brushed soundlessly, numbly, past. Surface anaesthesia was complete. Wild raspberry and thistle bounced harmlessly off my legs; nettles—the bane of an evening river-swimmer—bowed obsequiously.

It was curious to step into the black rushing water and feel no change at all; to stand, up to the waist, balancing precariously on an unseen slab, while strapping on a fin, and notice only lightness of the legs and cold water on the hands. The rest of the body was warm and sweatily damp, for the walk had been brisk.

Deeper in, and a slow cool tickling of the legs announced entry of lower water; then a searing chill flashed down my back, curled round, and clawed my belly—the zip had not been pulled high enough—before settling to comfortable coolness. I tightened the zip, held on to two boulders with outstretched arms, raised floating legs and lay back on the current, lifted and lapped by dimly felt water coursing beneath me. All other bodily sensation ceased, for hands soon adjusted themselves to warmth and I was this time wearing a hood. Loosing hold, I was washed into an eddy and circled there slowly with leaves and stems below thin hazel bushes, gazing up at the moon through a rotating filigree of branches. I must have floated there a full half hour, profoundly relaxed, almost asleep, beneath the increasing moon.

Emergence was squelchy, the gait dropsical and erratic, and pints of warm water spilled out on the doorstep; but it was clear I had gained almost as much with this extra skin as I had lost by muffling my own.

44

Peeling off the suit, is, as I have remarked, as bad as putting it on. I still find the best way to remove the breeks is to leap about until the last clutch is kicked off. This performance is naturally for a private place and if you emerge on a crowded beach or at a harbour there is nothing for it but to walk to some seclusion. Usually one has arranged for a car to be waiting at such a spot or, better, a van in which to change. Publicity is irritating, but has its amusing side. I remember coming ashore one evening at St Andrews, slopping through silenced groups of golf-chatter to a small parked car, then producing a mysterious key (actually from under a front tyre), shaking off most of the salt water, getting in and driving away; leaving disbelieving eyes with only a damp road to mark my brief apparition. I circled the Royal and Ancient in the dusk and drove to a friend's flat, to change. He was throwing a party and my somewhat dramatic entrance was taken as all part of the fun: 'Hang up your fins, old man, and have a drink.' So this I did, and remaining warm and sodden within became caressingly dry and smooth without. I was something of a pet seal, in fact, and the evening passed agreeably enough. It was well after midnight before I performed a belated and unsteady dance in the bath, and finally prised off the steamy neoprene.

In winter there is no obviously increased cooling through the suit. Leaks are unbearable, though, and exposed parts of the body suffer badly. I entered a large rapid river early one spring without hood or gloves, for the sun was clear and warm, celandines were gold in the birch woods and anenomes whitening into blossom. The surrounding hills were losing snow rapidly, so that the water, bright and fast, was scarcely above freezing point. Hands went rapidly numb, but this was merely an inconvenience. On diving I met the real trouble. My face shrank and pain punched my forehead. Icicles fingered suddenly-thinned hair and wrinkled my scalp. My neck froze to the base of my skull; I felt cold blood sniffing my spine. Out! I lost no time in scrambling on to the absurdly warm moss of the bank, and collecting hood and gloves. But I could not put them on; my hands were insensible and stiff.

I had to go and seek assistance from an old lady at a near-by cottage. My paralysed face and rubber lips made communication difficult and of course I could not feel, let alone hold, a pencil to write reassurance and explain that no one was drowned, or had fallen from a space-craft. Calmed eventually by my elaborately undramatic gestures, she laid aside the telephone and began to understand.

With hood and gloves safely on, I returned, warmed myself up and had no further trouble from the cold water; but my early chilling had cost me too much energy and the swim had to be cut short. One should certainly take no risks in winter.

The old lady had cause to feel apprehension, for one's appearance at a front door in such a suit *is* somewhat odd. In spite of the publicity given to police frogmen, and of the similar apparel worn by the more familiar water-skiers, one can still cause embarrassing surprise and finger-pointing by wearing a wet-suit out of aquatic context; much as, in the old days, an ice axe in the hand or a pair of skis on the shoulder swivelled all heads at an Edinburgh tram-stop. I avoid crowds on principle, and try to slip down to the water as rapidly and secretly as I can; all the more as prolonged walking in neoprene rubs the skin, and of course in hot weather one is stewed in sweat.

Yet encounters will occur. I remember the first day I walked along to a near-by river, down a small country road for about a mile. I was wearing the whole outfit very self-consciously, wrapped in a home-made weight-belt of Laocoon design, dangling a glittery camera, fins, mask, snorkel and carrying, of all things, a large rucksack full of clothes and towels; also, I had on Wellington boots, to save my neoprene slippers from the rough gravel. I looked, and felt, more than odd, on a dusty road in the sun, among birds and bees, tormentil and dry heather; I prayed I would meet nobody. But at the last bend I saw the local roadman, sitting in the grass chapping away at his shovel (it was a hot day); he was too preoccupied to look up as I approached. Gloomily sweating, I clomped on, trying to assemble some suitably facetious remark. Only when I was almost level with him did he look up. Not a twitch of an eyelid, not a muscle moved when he saw this astonishing sight in the middle of his road. He merely nodded ... 'A graund day ...' and resumed the chap, chapping away on his shovel, the noise fading as I went down the hill. There are still gentlemen in the world.... Then came the river and it was I who was sensibly clad, warm and lissome in an element where dungarees, tweeds or aprons were laughably, outrageously incongruous.

One other advantage of a wet-suit soon became evident, especially on long sea trips, one of an amusingly animal nature. It had always seemed prodigal to pass heat out, every few hours, at the bladder's command, into the unappreciative ocean. Now there is no trouser zip on neoprene breeches and undressing at sea for such a minor recurrent purpose is much less defensible, on grounds of energy conservation or of human dignity, than, say, dressing for dinner on safari. I need not linger on this particular advantage, nor on the doubtless Freudian origin of its satisfactory nature; but one found great material comfort in not squandering such a store of heat. Calculation suggests a complete sea-wash beneath the rubber every hour at the most, so that personal habits need never have long been called in question. Certainly any such qualms could never exist among wind and waves and clutching depths and, encountered afterwards, appear comic.

Because of the lightness of expanded neoprene and the air trapped with the suit, one's buoyancy is increased. I found, when surface swimming, that kick strokes became wasteful, threshing more air than water, for legs floated so high. Diving was frustrated: the bottom swam up to you, hesitated, then retreated despite frantic appeals. Without vigorous arm movement any submersion was impossible. As I had bought the suit primarily to be able to loiter below the surface, camera in hands, such buoyancy would obviously defeat my purpose.

A rubber belt threading two great slabs of lead had therefore to be worn. Buckled on, it made journeys to sea across weed and rocks much more deliberate; a slip or lean off balance could not be rectified, and rising from each heavy

47

collapse, clutching fins and mask and camera, became weari-some. All the greater was the relief of passing the weight to the water when at last you entered it; all the more desirable this sympathetically accommodating element.

Once in the sea, the weight had comparatively few draw-backs. The suit's airiness was effectively neutralized. Diving be-came effortless again, and the descent sustained; rising appeared unhindered. On the surface, fins worked in the water once more. Noticeably slower, though, was acceleration and, once moving, impetus increased dramatically, so that a few strong kicks at entrance would carry one leisurely across a silent rock-encircled bay, heavy and unhurried, regal as Leviathan.

In the less dense fresh water, well-adjusted sea ballast is too heavy; I remained buoyant enough to keep the tube above water when resting at the surface, but journeys from below required persuasion and had to be started earlier. It was always worth while to cast a weight.

I became reconciled to the rubber skin and developed sys-tems of communication through it. Some, at least, of the teem-ing messages that thrill through the water can be received again. Warmth and cold are not utterly cut off; I still have sensitive hands to explore them, and eyes to detect changes in refraction—shimmerings out of focus as threads of different temperatures intermingle. Vibrations, and even tex-tures, pass through the neoprene, animating the delicate water film and so the receptive skin, skin that is now warm and alert. As a blind man may detect change of colour with his sensitive hands, so I, along my rubbered body, can feel coarse rushes or soft grass among the lakes, smooth granite or rough schist beneath the rivers, the pull and counter-pluck of sea-eddies, the lithe straps of laminarians and horny thumbs of wrack; and can feel barnacles painfully enough, may even have to heal their stabs at night—by torchlight in a tent—with scissors and gum.

So much for keeping warm. Another question often asked concerns time. 'But you have so little time to be down there. How frustrating it must be. How long *can* you hold your breath?'

48

Such an outlook is irrelevant. Firstly, one is not always even looking 'down there'. Lazing on the surface, you never worry about down there. You can turn and see it any time, enter it any time. Meanwhile you revel in the up here. You have your double vision. Secondly, when you cruise along the coast you may, if you wish, spend hours, eyes submerged, virtually never ceasing to look down there; 'down there' seeps into you, mile after mile of it; and occasional dives are merely to focus up one particular aspect, performed unconsciously as one swings a zoom microscope to higher power at some interesting point on the slide, or twists the range of binoculars nearer or farther when combing a likely hillside for a stag. Thirdly, you never need to suspend breathing beyond a minute or a minute and a half, and usually the interval is much less. There is the well-known observation that skilled spear-fishers dive, find their fish, follow it, aim, kill it and return to the surface on an average of well under a minute of clock time. A period spent this way or, as I spend it, exploring below, is not commensurate with clock time, which is surface time.

I have already suggested the strong hypnotic effect of underwater scenes and motion, of the suspension of land-learned reactions, of the necessary extension—and to some extent replacement—of intellect by more primitive means of grasping the environment. With all this readjustment how can chronometric, mechanically ticked, time retain its measure? Often, jammed against some rock or clutching some stem far down, have I gazed up at the surface, seen slow shoals emerge and pass, black against the silver, and wondered detachedly how 'long' I have been down, and have examined with mild interest my heart-beats; and been surprised that after this apparently vast period of submergence I still have no desire to breathe in, just to loose a bubble or so. And then later, perhaps, after attention has been fixed for some time on movement and nosings in the undergrowth not far away, the signs do come: a feeling of deficiency in the chest, little feet pattering through earways with messages for the brain. And reluctantly, but automatically, do arms unclasp, feet push out, and I rise

49

to the expected surface, blow, breathe in—not very deeply —a few times, and come down again. But an observer, perched on his rock, watch-clutching, has ticked off scarcely a minute.

The signs begin in plenty of time, when you are at ease under water; they have to, for there may be emergencies delaying your cast-off for the surface, and at absolute breath-limit this journey upward has its own dangers. As you ascend, carbon dioxide floods out of the tissues—into which the pressure has forced it—back into the lungs where at the same time the small amount of available oxygen falls markedly; because consciousness depends on keeping the oxygen: carbon dioxide ratio high, there is always this small crisis to surmount on the way up. If ascent is accidentally delayed this normally insignificant hazard becomes more real; so it is fortunate that our reflexes allow us a little extra time to deal with an emergency.

There could be stiffened fingers to wrench from a grasp, a slipping fin to pull on tightly or—grave carelessness that an alert body never lets go unnoticed until so late—a jammed foot. More likely is the imminent loss of a valued object left behind among weed—I fought back for a dropped camera viewfinder this way, with heroic and foolish success. Such emergencies may entail a good few extra seconds, even half a minute, together with anxious activity to deplete your oxygen further, but that time is granted when you are, as I said, easy in the water. This immediate action for release or retrieval is performed rapidly and smoothly with no panic: or so I have found. Probably if carelessness has been mortal and no release is possible, panic may disperse the final moments; but it is difficult to be sure, for we know how well-attested are those calmly detached 'last seconds' of men apparently falling down mountains to their death, and who survived to tell their tale. Certainly in none of my few underwater emergencies did panic threaten because of short-age of breath, and experiences of friends faced with apparently inevitable drowning seem to agree with the objective accept-ance of the falling mountaineer.

I wrote that signs give ample warning, when you are at

ease. Occasionally, without being in any stress or danger, you are not at ease. You may, for example, be wrapped in the trials of underwater photography and, cursed with mechanical contraptions and calculations, never notice until almost too late the urgent knocking of your reflexes, and may even try to resist them; but I shall deal with these deserved embarrassments later. Or you may, as I have hinted before, be rather too much at ease, disembodied, fairly mesmerized and dreaming; then you never hear the signs; the automatic release and rise to surface begins in spite of you—so that you wake, suddenly apologetic and attempting to regain the controls, when you are already half-way up to rescue. The animal sanity of your carcase hauls it back and for the time being you had better follow. It is difficult, as well as indiscreet, to drown peering through eternity's keyhole.

The greater hazards of water pressure scarcely concern us in our thirty feet or so of depth. Increased weight of water outside is balanced by increased pressure of body fluids within, and we never notice the change. We avoid goggles because the air they enclose remains at surface pressure and below about ten feet the increased blood-pressure may burst small blood vessels around the eye; a mask prevents this bleeding because you can hardly help puffing air into it through the nose and so equalizing pressures inside and outside the eyes. Air volume in the lungs is of course easily adjusted by the flexible rib cage. These processes and many others are performd automatically; only in deeper waters, with aqualungs, may you have to concentrate upon your physiology.

Finally, to treat one other question often asked: 'Surely the water is never clear enough to see much—especially in these days?' Obviously, one picks only water that is clear enough, though it is surprising how many fogs resolve themselves at the bottom, provided sufficient light comes through. Even with visibility restricted to three feet an interesting time may be had down there, but of course you lose the space and glitter and have difficulty at first in finding the bottom at all. Such places must be reasonably free of current, for you have no means of estimating your motion relative to the bottom as you go below and may land many yards away from your intended touch-down and remain unaware of it; even in calm foggy water it is difficult, without watching bubbles, to keep descending vertically and the lift seems a long time going down before the doors slide apart at the ground floor. Ascent is easier, if you have enough air both to raise you and provide guiding bubbles, and if you have a firm flat bed to kick off from.

But cloudy water is not usually encountered off rocky or pebbly shores such as those of the West and North Highlands, Cornwall or parts of Wales. Even sandy places, provided they are far enough from a town and a recent storm has not stirred up the shoreline, are clear enough, especially in the north. Twenty or thirty feet of clear vision, with hazy outlines at fifty or more, are frequent enough off the West Highland coast; if not so saturated with light as that around Hawaii, such water is certainly more transparent to the eye than is the blue wash of the northern Mediterranean. Off the sandy east coast of Scotland in good light one could read—if the necessary arrangements were made—the regulation motor car number plate at twenty feet or so; though even with such figures blurred beyond twelve feet the scene is still clear enough for enjoyment, close objects—your main concern—being quite sharp and the periphery a colourful daub out of which a strange creation may at any time unfold itself.

Lowland rivers and lakes have usually poor visibility, for they lie in rich country. The nourishment available in these eutrophic waters allows vast populations of microscopic life and their swarming predators; through such dancing multitudes you fumble despairingly, following the pale gleam of your leading hand. Sometimes limbs and body are visually amputated; only the head remains, seeking consolation above the surface. Increasing wash-out of agricultural fertilizers is spreading this cloudiness. Over the last ten to fifteen years the lower reaches of many Highland rivers, draining through hill farms and forestry land, have yearly appeared to collect more green algae on their stones and more colourless fur; the sediment in their pools increases and the time taken for them to clear after disturbance grows longer.

Much more striking is similar 'pollution' following release
of sewage effluent (doubtless suitably treated beforehand) into
waters around heavily commercialized tourist areas. One river
I know has been changed—during the last five years—from a
fast golden throat of peat water, with bubbles and light
flashing over its polished boulders, to an equally rapid turmoil
of algae, sludge and paper fragments—an intimidating blizzard. Winter washes it; 'Some lucky day each November',
as Robinson Jeffers observed of elsewhere, '. . . the old granite
forgets half a year's filth.' Certainly from June to October the
outflow from hotels and camp-sites along its upper reaches
has already destroyed it for pleasurable swimming, and any
winter clarity it may possess between ice and spates is now
threatened by the growth of skiing in its neighbourhood. The
future of such easily exploitable areas may be guessed at.

Again, Loch Morlich was once one of the most wonderful
of Highland lochs, unique in its shallowness and clarity.
Patterned across the rocky hollows of its sun-dappled bed
lay great pine trunks, and pale green clusters of milfoil and
other aquatic plants spired thinly to six or seven feet. One
swam through woodland glades uncannily resembling the
great forest of Rothiemurchus itself. Now, following 'development' of this region, the water is a thin soup, polyzoa dancing
in its sun shafts. The yellow ropes of weed are furred and
the pebbles piles of mouldering biscuit; torn paper lolls in the
depths. However sparkling a sewage effluent may have been,
it remains too nourishing; algae and the flagellates will thrive,
but that limpid granite water, clear as a Cairngorm evening,
has gone for ever.

The change in such environments is not restricted to the
more-publicized terrestrial misfortunes, such as treading-out
of vegetation and erosion of summit slopes; the whole bio-
sphere, below as well as above the surface, is, in these rare
oligotrophic places, peculiarly sensitive to the pressures of
human population.

But there still remain fresh waters elsewhere we can enjoy
—a surprising number all over the British Isles. Let us visit
them.

# 6
## *About rivers and burns*

Fresh water is so different from salt. Islanded or elbowed by the land, it lacks the effortless power and self-sufficiency of unlimited ocean; its creatures are more apologetic and furtive, many of them on loan from the air or the encroaching soil. Land obtrudes everywhere. The water slips or fights a way through it; or, besieged, gathers in dull aquiescence, dreaming of ultimate horizons.

We shall begin with rivers. They exist only for the sea, or for some vast lake that will pass for a temporary sea. They move always towards it, by rage or by cunning, and when you swim long in rivers you also come to desire this consummation. It is possible to suppose them merely part of the sea, its fingers up and over the land; but experience will change your view.

Swim along the coast, pick out the estuary of a small mountain river—the larger slow ones are too muddily uncertain to tell you much until you are some distance up them—and make your way along it for the first mile or so. You know when you are approaching the mouth of such a small river—like the many in the West Highlands—by a change in the sea-light. If the river is very small, a mere burn, the blue and green distances retire to a pale amber, the weeds themselves shade to brown. At the burn mouth—a shallow scoop in the sea bed—a peaty haze is gathered. Moving into, and up, this scoop you feel a new force: a growing, unfamiliar, resistance. It may be warmer or colder, depending on the weather over the land (for in all things rivers reflect the moods of the land) but it is very different from a tide-thrust, being thinner and more persistent, like an invisible shoal pushing past you to the sea. Gone are the resplendent towers of kelp, so confident in oceans; slime and shoddy, dirt-sieving, are collected behind pebbles, and grass-like weeds, equivocally aquatic, sprout from the mud.

Mud. On the approach to a larger river, mud lies everywhere. Light stains in through high brown glass, powdered with drifting motes as in a neglected cathedral; picked out fitfully are dusty stretches of level floor, punctuated by boulders. All, boulders, pebbles and mud, possess an evanescent fur of algae and sediment. Your every movement disturbs this tilth, your approach unsettles it; it begins to sway before you, around your face it dances, prickling your ears, beneath you it is frantic and behind you, as your limbs beat it, there unwinds a coiling three-dimensional wake like slow smoke from a ship's funnel, spreading and unwinding pallidly into the gloom.

Diving is therefore not rewarding. Hands plunge into a warm broth, thickening to porridge at the elbow but prudently abandoned before then. On the surface you notice the slow abdication of sea, the unhurried enclosure by land. It is pleasanter to float in these places, flat as the interchangeable horizons of mud and water, remarking the bosomy cumulus overhead and the intricate spirals of bird flight; but for luxury one is tempted back to the maternal salt, to the complacent amplitude of its waves.

Few things are more enjoyable in a river than beating up a fast stretch, heaving from boulder to boulder against the spray, fighting up small falls and rapids. But rivers should be entered high up and followed down if one wishes to live them to the full. Travelling downstream is easier, but that is not its main attraction.

Following a river down its course is the more satisfying because you share its accession of strength, acknowledge each new thrust of tributary, triumph each mile over the withdrawing land and at the end relax in the water's total victory. We shall in fact go down such a river when we come to discuss touring; but let us begin, as I did, by going up, and by going up a hill burn—not so small and shallow as to preclude all swimming, but still a burn, indefinably definable as a burn and not a river: rivers know where they are going, burns never do until they find their river.

Looking at such a burn from its banks, pushing aside the rowan branches, one sees sunlight dappling across pebbles, nervous as an animal's skin; surfaces of black or silver sheeting the occasional pools; and always a running scroll of broken water between boulders and along rims and shallow turnings.

The course of a hill burn climbs dramatically upward in rocky steps, white where the water pours over or crowds between them; the steps continue downstream, vanishing round the next crooked bend, and the whole course is cluttered with rolled boulders and the collapse of stony banks. However unpromising for swimming, a squeezed visit is an underwater experience not to be missed.

Entering a suitable stretch, thigh-deep, say, over pebbles, you instantly discover the current with which you will always have to live. Your fins curl before it, your legs are nudged aside. Equally rapidly you discover the importance of hands; fingers must clutch and fins beat if you are not to slip away downstream, to be grounded at the edges or to rattle backwards among lower boulders. As you will see, all that live in these shallow running waters cling or swim. No floating progression here; the gale blows too hard.

Cling then, against the blast, and gaze underwater; and what you see recalls a summit boulderfield swept by continual wind, for there is no vegetation, only polished stones crouched against the flow, smaller ones crowded in their lee. The colours too are of the high plateaux. Above, the surface spins past in torn clouds of gold and silver; below, the sun flickers and moulds itself incessantly on the pebble mosaic in every shade again of yellow, amber and gold; the surrounding darkness bundles into the rock. Everything is shifting, there is no sense of rest; your body streams out behind, pulled, plucked, ready to go too but for the white fingers clenched beside you. Ceaseless also the stream of noise, the rattling of bubbles and the flat echo of an occasional dislodged stone, measuring its one length nearer the sea.

Inevitably your eyes search upstream for the source of this

power. The floor stretches ahead, squatting here and there in pools and interrupted by blocks, the taller ones brushed with bubbles; and farthest ahead, where the luminescent peat-water purples into darkness, there swings a kind of dimly lit candelabra, a cluster of glass beads. You draw yourself forward from handhold to handhold, feet helping—an amphibious progression in keeping with this crawling landscape so tunnelled by water—towards that light, now expanding into a swarm of bubbles. It is the bottom of a waterfall.

Waterfalls, however tiny, are the delights of running water. In this burn they were the best places to visit, above or below the surface. Usually they emptied into a pool, scooped by them in some excess of spate. These pools were cratered down to darkness, and rimmed by boulders still tremulous after their last drubbing. Handing off this unstable debris, one glided out of the tug of current into the scoop's relative calm; there, curled against a bed-rock whose angularities had been smoothed by long experience of storms, one could lie and watch the ceaseless play of bubbles, listen to the beat and throb of their myriads, and follow the occasional leaf or twig in its short bewildered trajectory among them.

Yet to lie long in such burns is cramping. They are useful for afternoon splashes in warm water if nothing else is near, but no substitute for the rivers themselves. We can rise and follow this particular burn upstream a little, slipping and sliding among its rocks, reaching up slimy runnels, wading gravelly shallows; a progress you may think surely easier in gumboots or, even better, ashore along its heathery flanks —except that by swimming or hauling wherever possible you remain faithful to the water, so that when after half a mile or so you breast its last battlement and enter a broad upland corrie, it can reward you with the relief of a plunge into its relaxed meanderings there.

Now little more than a ditch, man-deep and scarcely five feet wide, its black waters are strangely clear. Light shafting through the colloidal peat is confused to fluorescence, but the shadows remain sharp. Among them, trout flash blackly. The bed is rubbery boulder clay smoothed by centuries of slow

57

current, humped occasionally with mouldering slabs of ancient banks, collapsed and heeled over long storms ago. This dark corridor is curtained at intervals by weeds, lush fresh-water growths quite different from plants of the sea. They are rooted in the mud, they possess roots, gleaming like teeth when disturbed. Their stems, bright silver-green stems of land plants, celery-white below, supple and confident, seek up to the light. Their flat rushy leaves lie along the surface, drinking sun, or float there in complacent cups. More truly aquatic vegetation, milfoils and *Nitella*, cringes characterless among them.

It is strangely refreshing to slide between these creaking stems, parting them gently, writhing the body—for movements more violent than such insinuations would provoke breakages, entanglements, clouds of rising mud—while ahead of you, slow but always keeping ahead, move little packs of troutlets. When you rest, cosseted among green juices, the fish return, and the small animals—beaded beetles and larvae, legged and frilled—appear and resume their business. Pond-skaters gather and inspect your emergent knees.

Clouds sail high across blue sky; wind visits from the corrie shoulders, combs the long tussock grass above you without touching the surface and vanishes to invisible upper moorlands. You lie in a tiny vein of water. Land is the norm, a sea not credible.

The large rivers believe in the sea. Fanatic, they roar past you, striking at boulders, lunging over crags, boiling with intolerance. They must be entered with caution. The wind here may be a hurricane. One must learn with the fish.

Enter therefore behind a large projecting boulder where the trout must lie; one crowned with turf or perhaps a young rowan, and sprinkled with ferns tossing in the air blast. The water below it is calmer, smooth, circling quietly, and laps a gravelly shore. Beyond it, the current races past but out there—and as far as can be seen downstream—only a few white heads appear above the broad wrinkled irritation: there

*(1a)*: Beginning a sea tour (p. 129). Entering a shallow bay in Benderloch carrying mask and fins and wearing a quick-release belt with lead weights and sheath-knife. The route lies out with the ebbing tide through the wrack, into deep water over sand and then round the headland to the right.

*(1b)*: Camp by the West Highland sea. Inside the tent hot soup is brewing for the swimmer coming home on the tide. Days of fine swimming can be enjoyed from places such as this without needing to walk further than from sleeping-bag to shore. *(Photo: Tom Weir)*

(2a): Shark? No, his own fin lazily creaking the surface as the swimmer basks in calm waters on the way back from a trip down the Firth of Lorne (p. 121). The peace of isolation some quarter of a mile out from deserted shores.

(2b): A pause in the late afternoon of a long day off the Argyll coast, to eat jam sandwiches from a pre-arranged cache. Note how perfect at ease one sits, half-floating in the warm wrack. A few minutes more, and the swimmer will gently push off, back up the coast on the incoming tide.

(2c): Hauled out at low tide on a skerry for an air-bathe during a trip along the north coast of Ardnamurchan. The hard rock is strange, but the water and weed-thongs blend with your neoprene limbs. To slip off into the waves is irresistible – for a hundred yards out lie the great underwater laminarian forests.

A colour sequence, giving on paper only a poor image of the brilliant reality (see p. 99).

3a): A picture snatched from the bucketing crest of a wave, with the bright green island of Lismore visible for an instant before you slide back into the gurgling trough. A glorious day of sun and sparkle among pleasantly jostling waters.

3b): Going down. ... Beneath the waves lie calm, silent forests of weed. The swimmer cruises just above them, free of time and space. Note the bubbles issuing from the snorkel tube as breath is slowly released, and the utterly relaxed posture.

3c): Down in the forest. A dogfish embosomed in laminarian thongs and doubtless wishing it were shark enough to scare away the intruder. (Taken by natural light some twenty feet down off Moidart.)

3d): Shallow waters among groves of wrack in Loch Linnhe, as the swimmer moves out to deeper places. It is low tide, for the wrack floats only at half mast, and the direction of its tail indicates the course and strength of the ebb – all important signs to be watched by the ever-careful explorer.

Two views of a highland river.

*Above (6a):* To clamber down such waterfalls and then slip softly into pools beneath (p. 124) is to savour the best of the upper stretches of a river like the Orchy . . . *(Photo: R. M. Ad*

*Left (6b):* . . . and then to dive in these pools and, looking up from t potholes, to see great salmon circling to the surface like 'moths round a flame, light stroking their satin backs', is to begin to know y river at last. Such sights are difficu to film: the photographer here stalked his prey with an aqualung the Aberdeenshire Dee. *(Photo: Iain Ros*

Quiet evenings.

*Above (7a)*: A lowland river. The English Dee, a long, inviting gallery 'alder-edged and fly-haunted, with a smooth black surface exquisite to press apart' (p. 14).

*Below (7b)*: The mountain waters of Loch Assynt, offering only reeds, rocks and the mountain sky – islanded and timeless, known only to the lonely evening swimmer. *(Photo: R. M. Adam)*

*(8)*: The Golden Skerries. Looking to Coll and Tiree – or anywhere out west, the Scillies or to Ireland or imagined Labrador – across the evening waters. Impossible, surely, to clamber back on to that half-forgotten land. . . . Better to drift half an hour longer beyond those rocks until the moon comes up and cools it all to silver. *(Photo: R. M. Adam)*

are no waterfalls below you—they are upstream a little, where the rocky banks close in.

Submergence reveals the familiar amber glow, but larger gloomier boulders than in the burn lie here, heavily abandoned, the occasional skeleton of a drowned tree among them, trapped and rigid. Trout, translucently drab, shades of this underworld, shift together in threes and fours behind shelter, flitting from lee to lee through patches of gold.

The current must be tested warily—and on the surface. Clutch your boulder carefully, work round it, noting the swing and seethe of current, until you enter the welter at its outer edge. There your shoulders are tugged, legs pulled out and if you have poor fingerholds—they should have been good dry grabs, jug-handles—away you will go, whisked off, drawn backwards ever faster; so you will have to thresh furiously and elbow out of the procession, breaking back to the calm lee.

Once successfully round the boulder and confidence gained, you can drive upstream close to the bank, beating legs only; then stop beating, drift rapidly back, beat again, edge further out, feel the growing force of the current and the more powerful response of fins (and arms now) until you can thrash up the centre in a strong crawl and escape to shelter smoothly and at will.

Experience will teach when the river is likely to hammer too boisterously, and you can recognize its force from your shelter just as you judge the strength of a wind from the doorway before venturing out with an umbrella—leaves blowing, twigs moving, branches heaving, whole trees in turmoil; one assembles one's own Beaufort scale for this aquatic windscape. Such primary lessons are best learnt on a familiar stretch of river. Higher, whiter heads of spray, fiercer furrows in the surface, have counterparts below; if the flood is clear enough to peer underneath you see small stones shuffled along like cards, larger flat ones hopping intermittently from group to group through the flying gravel and, in waters from which you must retreat at once, dimly through the tornado great boulders teetering, lifting and falling

59

back on to scrambling pebbles as the blast catches them. But a mild flood is invigorating. Prudence when the river is known and caution when it is not, add a frame to the challenge; thoughtless plunge and attack is not only foolish and dangerous but grossly insensitive to the world you have chosen.

When you have fenced with your river for long enough, so that you can thrust upstream, streak downstream, curve and circle, cross it and drift it, landing where you wish, then you may begin to dive. You might have glanced underwater before this, but the first swimming in rapid shallows—especially down-current—needs sharp eyes above water; for a blow on the head from an unseen rock can stun, and that is trouble indeed.

You pick a large slow pool in which to dive, a greater version of the little spray-fed scoops along the burn. If you dive up-current there is of course more struggle, once down, to move along the bottom and hands may have to help by grabbing: they will certainly have to cling if you wish to stay down. When diving down-current, descent is a little easier but progress along the bottom is disconcertingly fast and rock barriers downstream approach frontwards or sideways with unexpected rapidity. So it is probably best to begin by diving upstream; then, with increasing skill, you may twist and somersault and spiral, harnessing the current, using it for your manoeuvres as the gull and the glider pilot ride their own shifting winds.

The most enjoyable of these acrobatics are beneath waterfalls, where you are plunged and tumbled in a thrilling shower of beads, where head and feet spin giddily among exploding crystal; and only when you are thrown or, breathless, swim clear into the sober gloom can you begin to see whether the surface lies below, above or to one side of you. Always in these places the arms protect the head, fingers spread and feel for warning; especially on the up-kick to the surface, for rock shelves frequently jut out from banks just below waterlevel. And always of course the floor of the scoop is examined first for such shelves or for protruding knives of rock or timber. Provided the out-run is unobstructed and one is easy in the water, then there is no under-tow or suck in a summer river that cannot be kicked away from, that cannot be swung out of, with an exhilaration like that of a climber revelling through overhangs, master of his craft.

Yet, as the soundest-looking ledge may heel away beneath your feet though stood on by hundreds before you, so there is always the possibility of the unforeseen swirl that spins you on to rock, cork-helmet or no; the second pull-down, at last gasp, by a current over a hidden shelf; the jammed limb. You may lose your axe, or your crampon, on a North Face: your fin may be forced off in fierce water. I have written of this before; when one steps on to the hill, into the water, behind the wheel, out of the nursery, dangers begin; choice and experience decide the rest, and fortune.

But let us away and search out the fish, shake free of these air torrents and glide into calmer waters. Yet if we do, if we dive to the far side of the great scoop beneath the falls, grip tight to some rock down there and look round this dim and uneasy bowl—with stray bubbles and twigs and caught-up debris from the floor still blowing about us—we see few fish. Camouflage does not explain this scarcity. Here and there, tilted within shadows, hang occasional grey shapes; but where are the great trout for which this river is famed?

Only when we paddle slowly back towards that billowing white curtain do we see them. Approaching from below, from the chest-bruising bottom boulders, we emerge out of emptying gloom into light, light drenching down in sheets and showers of brilliant air, galaxies whose lower fringe vibrates with separate bubbles. Let us watch the display this time, not rampage amongst it. There, shoulder to shoulder, nosing the refreshing shower, lie the big trout, holding still, shrugging the current aside, adjusting with the tail. At intervals one will peel lazily off to take some dark object bowled past from above, then resume his position; the others remain fixed and staring. The shoal drives ever forward, ever in the one place.

It is possible, having taken a good breath, to come up amongst them and hang with them in the teeth of the blast, airspray sharp on the face, eyes dazzled, clumsily groping for a handhold or pawing and kicking desperately to remain abreast. They move aside for you—as did the eels in their obsession—these trout hypnotized now by roar and spray, who are so lightning-wary back in the shadows; but I never found the same satisfaction beside them in such places as when flying with the elvers through space and time. Here there is effort, either to cling or to swim, a strain not shared by the fish. One is too anxiously clumsy; and although the turmoil of battered air fascinates, its belligerence keeps the body insistent, the sweep back into stony darkness behind is all too imminent; you dare never relax.

Such big falls are therefore best enjoyed as rough-and-tumbles among more dignified and capable inhabitants, and you may hitch on to the current any time and surge away downstream hounding the trout before you in schools that break apart—explode—at oncoming boulders, to re-form beyond them and fly on. At a furious pace you are borne downstream, past the evasive trout, needing every skill to dodge and parry, to fend off the obstacles flung at you up-wards and from either side until breathless you twist behind some more responsible rock and break out for air.

You find a great contrast. Tall green birches hang above; the banks relax, eternal couches of moss and fern. Time has suddenly stopped, and you have been flung into silence. Your head still sings from the violent movement and the noise you have left—the rumbles, rattles, beatings of great waterfalls, castanets of eddies. Around you now is a vast stillness, the river compressed to a murmur.

This double vision in rivers is disturbing. Whereas in the sea you had twin amplitudes complementary, making the great O continuous above and below its surface bisection, here you have a narrow roaring tunnel, a jolting tubeway, and above it instantaneous, illimitable calm. The shock of transition is at first dizzying. Only in quieter pools can you begin to comprehend the difference, and know that a river is water incomplete, racing to its fulfilment of sea through an incompatible land. The amber-gloomy tunnel, with its bare furniture of bed-rock and boulders, holds always the forebodings of a spate; only then, when floods ram down the whole shaking corridor, is the river fully employed. At other times, when you may swim in it, there is the feeling of early morning on the Underground, expectant before the rush hour; you wander between loose tons of rock paused in their journeying, visit great caverns gouged by past furies and still to be gouged by thousands more. An unreal and dilettante exploration, yet sufficient for you to come closer to rivers and understand why their double vision cannot satisfy. Only at the sea-beaches does the land achieve extinction and dignity; here it is unbearably complacent, and you turn back to the restless water.

Continuing downstream in shallower places is hazardous. Hands pass you on from stone to stone, pressing back your trundled body, your belly grates across slabs and gravel; occasionally legs are swung right round in front of you. Much writhing is needed to keep your course controlled and your head well clear of opportunist boulders. Then the fuss rattles away and you are launched on to a broad pool, where dives and waltzes are possible; like those places on a ski descent where after hundreds of feet of ice-rough gully, anxious with juddering slip and the flicker of rocks, the slope sighs out into a welcoming bosom of snow and the skier weaves hugely his own devices, curlicued with spray, celebrating liberty.

Certainly, swimming in rivers like this one, sucked by the sea's force of gravity, does resemble sport among the mountains. Yet if these rapid descents recall those on ski, you have here a freedom denied the skier—even with his skins and waxes—for by simply driving your legs you may surge at once uphill, no longer drunk with free descent but enjoying the sharp rewards of your own applied power; and know that at any time you may relax and, curving round, *schüss* downhill once more. Or you may continue forcing upward until you are scrambling, pushing up through shallows and—using elbows, shoulders, hips, knees and fins as well as hands— reach a smoother incline, very steep; beat up this, and find yourself beneath a rock wall pouring water. So a rock climb follows, and a wriggle through the summit spray lands you in an upper bowl, to forge through water further to the next obstacle, and so on. And then the return, down all these diversions, using every skill of eye and muscle and animal sharpness, until maybe a mile downstream, exuberantly exhausted, you are tossed aside into the chosen sandy alcove beneath the alders; and after the *taorluath* and the *taorluath a mach* and the *crunluath* with its mounting intricate excitement, you hear again the slow *urlar*, the clear ground of the pibroch, restoring all again to the origin.

So you lie there, swung gently by the current, gazing downstream over the shovelling water, downstream between the parted birches, mile after mile of shifting sun-dazzle gravelling down for hundreds, thousands of years, among uneasy earth and heaved rocks; and the river feeds through your bones, you feel it cold behind you from the great ice sheet, its first blustering through loosened moraines, through stranded whalebacks of sand; you hear its predecessors, rivers before the ice age, whispering down this glen through stranger, unfamiliar trees, echoes of rivers in glens here long since vanished, in landscapes long since powdered and rubbled away, buried or carried to sailed-off oceans, ice age beyond ice age; always that call downstream, the ceaseless abrasion, river-bed on river-bed, waters singing to an infinite glitter of seas.

Such is the dreaming beside your river after the chase and the battle, the same dream through many rivers, high-country ones, each following through familiar variations of rapid, shallow, cataract and pool its own subtlety of theme, threading the great drone of mountains, each with its own spirit, its own *ùruisg*, each to be courted separately but all rewarding, all draining today out of your bones, washing you remote as one of their pebbles, bright beside you here in the sun. No wonder the first men worshipped rivers.

Slower rivers, low-country ones, are usually too murky for any double vision but of course afford good surface swimming, preferable to creaking about in boats, and here it is best to go downstream alternately pedalling and freewheeling with the current. You drift a long progress down your Mississippi, a detached head observing unwinding banks, rafted on your own thoughts beneath the procession of trees. Silence is the attraction of such rivers, only the wind pawing at leaves far above; or, perhaps, framed in that silence and growing nearer as in a film close-up, a hoarse sibilance where the black flow parts to let some largely submerged trunk protrude, edged silver and, once passed, fading rapidly behind you.

Snags like these are hazards, but not serious when one is on the surface. Diving in such blind and unknown water is wrong because not only can you see nothing at all but it is again deliberate insensitivity, a challenge to the *ùruisg* and a treason to your animal intelligence bringing only relief, or conceit, at having come up again and missed unseen unnecessary danger: a Russian roulette of no relevance here.

To submerge the face in such dirty lowland water is anyway repellent; lips compress against its advances. Pleasures, like the hazards, are only taken in these rivers at the surface.

Rowing-boats or other river craft which you meet when you drift down by waterside villages or suburbs, as on the English Dee or upper Thames or Severn, are both pleasures and hazards. Pleasures, because passing among them—having announced your presence by kicking up white water (a head being to them mere flotsam)—you realize the extent of your water-change. You gaze up at a succession of peering faces, strange and indistinguishable as those of a Chinese crowd to a European; their bodies jerk and rattle in their husks of wood; they are dry and clothed. Words may be exchanged, but little else; for what comprehension have they of such a drifter from upstream, bound for his further miles of water? And how can you—just now—comprehend these boat-loads? To you they are mere incidents in a cavalcade, tableaux of a land-life you have relinquished, interesting only for their rapidly succeeding arrival and departure, each one similar; until they are gone, and the long gallery stretches on in more subtle formulations.

I remark later how the sea dehumanizes the swimmer, and

how salutary this is; and, as a necessary corollary, how still more salutary it is when he escapes from that clutch and thankfully returns to his fellow men. Here in these big slow rivers I believe this surrender to other powers comes with drifting on the current; much as, when once behind the wheel and committed to his engine, a normal humane citizen tends to regard pedestrians as minor irritants of a different and negligible species. They flit into vision, and are past. So do jay-splashing boaters appear to the travelling swimmer.

But he has to keep alert for them. Hazards are their poised and dripping oars, and the screws of their motor boats. These last may be heard thinly along the surface when far off, and underwater their sound is tiny and precise like the winding of a wrist watch, and its direction so uncertain that surfacing is as perilous as it is necessary. On the bigger rivers, near towns, large pleasure launches, fast and unmanoeuvrable, make the swimming I have described impossible, and darting and dodging come before anything else. The Rhine at Cologne—or anywhere below Schaffhausen—and the harbour at Marseilles are examples where most of the delight, perhaps all, is to play the matador and be swung aside by the huge outwash of a thunderous barge, or to predict—successfully—the erratic courses of hydroplaning power boats. You have little chance—no more than of understanding a countryside from a motor road—of savouring the river itself or the places along its banks; it is better to remain dry and sit behind the rails of a pleasure steamer if faced with such distractions.

In more swimmable rivers the most serious hazards I know of are fishing lines, nylon ones long caught beneath some rock in a deep salmon pool and their ends, many yards away perhaps, wrapped around a branch or boulder. Almost invisible, this web will string you to a halt and often I have had to back-paddle immediately and unwind the grip. Pulling is useless, for nylon will not break; it can only be cut rapidly by a sharp knife with a serrated blade, and one must always be carried.

But this jogs the memory: we have surely been swept a

66

long way from those fish we were chasing in Highland rivers. ... Let us go back to them. The smallest first. I never hunt fish underwater to kill them; rather to see them, see myself and see a little of what binds us together and where it comes from. But once I did catch a fish underwater, with my hands. I give this story to the manta-ray enthusiasts.

A small girl required a minnow for a garden pool. It had to be a minnow; a trout would grow to be too fierce, and eat up the other cherished inhabitants. I prowled the shallows, sieved the gravels, but only winnowed clouds of troutlets, each a potential murderer, a tyrant of the pond. As I was pulling ashore empty-handed, or rather carrying two empty nets—and swimming with them had been frustrating enough—I saw an undoubted minnow, sole representative of the thousands I had been assured haunted those gravels. On my approach it dived into deeper water. I followed this miniscule which, about five feet down, jumped into a small rusty can and stayed there, eyeing me balefully from just below the rim. With unusual presence of mind I abandoned the nets and grabbed the can, raising it above the surface so rapidly that the astonished fish had no chance to swim out. I proceeded to the shore bearing aloft the precious vessel, whose occupant, so far as I know, lived happily in his pond ever after.

The largest fish, the only 'fish', in these rivers, are of course salmon. Swimming the great salmon rivers, especially in a wet-suit, understandably alarms riparian owners or tenants and courtesy, if not prudence, requires you to ask their prior permission. The upper Spey and Dee, bottomed by lazily moulded pink granite, bone-smooth, sweeping into beds and shoals of exquisitely multicoloured pebbles, are worthy haunts of such fish. Scattered about rudely are rusted tins and prongs, relics of clumsy—or quick-witted—poachers; do not raise them to the surface for examination or as souvenirs, for a keeper will inevitably be passing and explanations occupy time better spent beneath the surface.

Time spent as I spent it one day, moving upstream under the green crystal of the Dee. Late in the afternoon I came to the entrance of a deep pool and rested there below, on a raw pine log jammed in the narrows. Beyond, the river bed dropped to the blue base of the pool, the pale encircling walls elegantly traceried with sunlight.

In the centre of this bowl, round and round, swam some half dozen great, enormously great, silver fish, breath-catching in beauty, passing and re-passing from sun into deep shadow.

Light stroked their satin backs, glinted on the flexing armour of gills, on the hooks of those helmeted jaws. Only the red eyes swivelled; the pectoral fins flickered; the haunches shuddered. Otherwise they processed in heraldic immobility, commanded by the ages. This ritual, embedded deep in the green Dee, stirred up forgotten prohibitions. I fingered the shredded bark uneasily. To enter the pool would certainly be sacrilege. Yet I required air.

I therefore relinquished the log, drifted back downstream, and rose to the surface. Foolishly, I raised my eyes. Wind brushed silver through the upper pines. A dipper jerked along the bank. When I dived again, the spell had been broken; and the exertion must have coarsened me. I brutally crossed the threshold.

Like the crack of a whip the silver exploded away to darkness and was gone. There remained only the clear green light and honest, empty, granite shadows.

I have never seen salmon so splendidly again. Perhaps I have been unlucky or too unskilled or since that time under some ban, or perhaps I should have had an aqualung and lain in wait for them to come at their pleasure. I have been in pools with them, watched them leaping about me, flinging themselves at, and sometimes over, a low fall near my house, their bodies smacking heavily on the surface or—agonizingly to the watcher—against wet rock; but underneath the troubled water—fogged with grains of the mica-schist which here replaced clean granite—only vast pale shapes were visible, appearing and disappearing with unbelievable speed: the trout and I had to crouch aside. My attempts to photograph them were perilous and will be told of in due course. I have seen one photograph of these great fish which hints at their majesty; it was taken by a friend who lay with his aqualung at the bottom of a Dee pot-hole, while they circled far above his head, blue and gold against the surface, like heavy moths about the moon. Look at them on plate 6a.

These upward views from pot-holes are dramatic features of a riverscape. There was one narrow black shaft some fifteen feet deep—its walls only an arms'-stretch wide—near my home. It opened below a high thin waterfall and rocks thirty feet tall enclosed it except for a cleft disappearing downstream. Fierce spates and thaw loosened those walls and they crashed down one roaring night, so that nothing is visible now but a pile of spiked rubble proud of the foam, the top of a great cairn where there was once a deep pool. I used to descend—never dive—this pot-hole carefully, pulling myself down head-first hand over hand. Amongst its features were downward-set teeth of rock in the walls, facilitating such descent but making return to the surface a matter of head-shielding and accurate aim. Once down, I could squeeze among fallen blocks at the bottom and gaze up, watching the resident trout, scared into shadow by my descent, make their way back sniffing and cautious into the beam of light: where they hung silhouetted against the distant surface, which was small and agitated as a farewell handkerchief, like decoys in the jaws of a trap. Not all pot-holes appear so punitive; but I shall describe others later.

One soon recognizes the habits of various fish, especially the trout and salmon parr ubiquitous in rivers such as these. Returning often to the same river one meets what must be the same groups behind their favourite rocks, in the outfall of the upper current, waiting for prey to be swept by. In strange rivers one can forecast, more skilfully than a surface angler, in what shelters they will be lying.

This gives you an effective means of allaying the fears of any fisherman who sees you; his surprise being usually succeeded by suspicion that you are—illegally—spearing, or by irritation, for you 'will be sure to frighten the fish'. You will not frighten the fish; no more than temporarily, at any rate, in these waters. Even if chased, they will escape to re-gather, as soon as they can, behind you in their old feeding positions. Your presence—if for one moment allowed—in the velvet chalk-fed silence of a southern English trout stream might well send them to ground for longer. To reassure the angler you may tell him where his quarry is lying, how many, how big and so on. He will be appeased and, when successful through your advice, be embarrassingly profuse in thanks and in similar requests. Short of fastening the fish to his hook you can do no more, and I have sometimes been driven away by the importunities of eyeless fishermen previously helped in this manner.

Perhaps trout do not react so violently when strangers appear under the water instead of above it. At one pool I know well, an evening rise can be all but banished by a heavy-footed approach; yet I have swum there often among fish taking flies, watching them feeding at eye level all about me. Half-heartedly I tried to recognize the various types of rise described in angling texts. The 'slash', the 'head and tail' and the 'porpoise roll' appeared commonest, but from below in such varied tumbling waters a whole range of movement was observable, from an exuberant leap—the victor returning garlanded with bubbles—to an apathetic suck. In another pool, little-fished and very small, trout continued rising uninterruptedly amongst three children who splashed and shouted enough, for they were learning to swim. Perhaps one should fish with dry fly and wet suit.

There remain two aspects of rivers with which I am less familiar: rivers in spate, and rivers under ice. A mild spate, of peat and froth, chocolate and cream, along a safe stretch with an easy retreat down-current to well-padded banks, offers interesting exercise to the fit. The most furious efforts of leg and arm are needed to wrest even a few yards of way upstream, and continuous hard swimming keeps you in reasonable equilibrium with one particular rowan on the bank: a type of exercise otherwise performed in those wheels fitted to the cages of pet mice. Still, it is good to feel the muscles of your river. Never, of course, does one go downstream at such times, except possibly in parties clad with hard hats and soft cushions, a shouting slalom popular in some parts of the world and certainly promising thrills enough of participation and survival: but as it is essentially communal and organized, it does not concern us here.

Neither does one enter in a 'real' spate, even to peer round a boulder at the torrent going down—not in these rivers. Balance is easily lost beside such a vomiting foreground; eyes are whipped downstream, ears confused by the clamour. The banks shake dramatically enough; one may remain there and watch from above the intolerable power of those dizzying tons of flung water. All rocks are smothered; one single rope of foam is slung from bend to bend down the glen. Enough: such hurricanes permit no swimming—even the trout notch into shelter—and their horror and fascination have been excellently described in that classic of Sir Thomas Dick Lauder, *The Moray Floods*.

In contrast, I have once sailed in the silent frothless spate of a wide lowland river, heavy with rain and mud, along with tree trunks, planks and probably the lum hat itself; but this was accidental, due to the capsizing of a coxed four, and our attention was on preserving the priceless boat. I recall the leg-warming massage of powerful water, but as heads were never risked under such thick cocoa and hands never left the gunwale we need not record anything beyond the rapid approach and dispersal of tree-clad horizons and a detached contentment in accelerating like this at head-height with the river; the stretch of water ahead gleamed like the long bonnet of a contemporary Lagonda, and the river banks flew past very satisfyingly. Fear I can't remember, only a growing horror at the inevitable damage when we would at last have to wake up and guide our arrowing projectile against the side of the school pontoon, now not far away. As it was, we tangled in mooring ropes and slowed to a pleasurable anti-climax, while the flood surged on without us.

After an upland burn or river has been in spate its profile will have changed. Falls are pushed downstream, filling up their old pools and scooping out new ones below; boulders are trundled to a fresh heap. Banks of pebbles have been shifted here, and curtains of gravel pulled across there. A hazel has been torn from the bank, its roots releasing rocks for a new weir; they slant across the current, sharp with edges and fresh-cracked colour. Even if the scene above surface remains little altered, beneath it there must have been changes, familiar stones being moved a foot or so nearer to the Atlantic or the North Sea; their smooth skin is broken with rolling, chipped by collisions or by the blizzard of smaller fragments. After a great spate, exploring old stretches underwater is like wandering in a well-known wood after a spring gale; there is a curious shamed silence while unfamiliar objects slowly assert themselves; gaps are revealed, and one recognizes further away, incomplete and grouped quite differently, constituents of a time now gone for ever.

Between the big spates of autumn and spring, these rivers suffer ice. I have never swum beneath river-ice, but I have been in the water with ice, and have watched carefully enough the process of freezing in Highland burns and rivers.

However cold it may be early in the winter—and I have known it 11° F in November beside the river at my house—the earth has not cooled enough for rapid waters to freeze. Protruding stones may sugar with rime or shrink below verglas, small pot-pools may be crack-plated thinly or ice-rimmed, but the main bed runs black through the surrounding snow.

Later, by mid-December in a cold year, the frost bites the river bones. The slow pools freeze in plaques, cracked where they hinge, lifting and falling with the water level and crisped with meringues of foam. In fast-running water ice begins on the rocks—at the sides, in mid-stream and on the bed. These rocks are well below freezing point and the film of water nearest them is slow enough to congeal; then the film passing over it, and so on. In this way ice grows out in mushy clusters and wide shallow rapids freeze upwards from the bottom. Brims of waterfalls build themselves up, their gaps pack tight, and behind them levels rise, brown drowning the white; below them levels fall and the water echoes glassily beneath abandoned vaults. Boulders become encased in frozen spray and this blue-shadowed rigor paralyses entire chains of cascades. Pieces slide and splinter off suddenly.

In the strange fragmenting silence you feel an interloper. The water has turned in on itself and is changing. You are not welcomed at this metamorphosis, nor is any living thing: water is returning to rock. You sense the blunt hostility of a glacier. There is no hold to grip, nor surface on which to lean; you are deflected instantly.

Wading amongst this frigid statuary you dislodge slobs of underwater sponge-ice, which heel over and reluctantly journey away, jamming together at constrictions; these dams raise levels behind you and so strain the ice plates of upper pools, cracking and displacing them. This melancholy slump and gurgle, punctuated by rending and sighing, does not add to one's courage in such places and I confess my aquatic excursions have been largely vertical (in intent if not—because foothold is so uncertain—in execution). Otter tracks stroll confidently off the snow and vanish into black openings, re-appearing farther upstream; red stains and a few scales record each triumph. An otter has excellent fur, an effective tail (its winnowing of the snow is very evident) and moreover needs to do this sort of thing. I myself have never yet gone beyond short immersions in clear areas, with quick glances into the dimness under ice.

Ice from below is jewelled with frozen bubbles like old blown glass and these distorting panes are ribbed and fused to the foundation rocks by white pillars, fluted and mysterious in the olive light; but the unyielding, punishing, hardness of ice makes long experience very necessary before venturing under it. So I have only nibbled round the edges of great pools as yet but partly frozen, stiffly gloved and helmeted, admiring the sun on white static waterfalls; down these, in runnels of blue and green, crept that part of the river still at liberty. More daring, I have floated out beside crags daggered with ten-foot icicles, body-thick, and clasped their blades delicately; icicles of this kind will project beneath the surface if an ice-jam has raised river-level, and down them sunlight probes into lifeless clear black water, apparently devoid of fish. The hush of this usually so boisterous scene subdues one further.

Perhaps more experience will allow the old spontaneity, but I think not. With so much of the surface false or unpredictable the double vision has gone, and one may peer and explore but never join unthinkingly with this environment: certainly not if one is alone. Yet exploration brings its rewards, then and later. To clamber carefully out, frictionless, on to glassy rocks through a tinsel of shore-crust in the red evening light, black boughs above you locked in white, and to pad home across the snow, the black wet patches on your rubber congealing to dullness and then to grey, slipping off in icy berries as you walk, is satisfying; and pictures of this river and of the other frozen rivers of the world flood their cold correction into the all-too-easy summer memories.

Much may be learnt from rivers, along their paths and seasons.

*Note.* The light perforated plastic helmets sold for canoeists are advisable when exploring fast and rocky rivers. They interfere very little with one's manoeuvres.

# 7
# *About lochs and pools*

Fresh water has other attractions, when it is islanded. There is quietness again, after the river's hammering, and a softness in broad water shielded from the sea's salt and bite. Its lower density admits you gladly, and there is no current to nag. You sink without protest.

In large deep lochs this calmness causes sharp stratification of temperature. With no significant current or waves the sun-warmed upper layers do not mix with the cold body of the water and the boundary between them remains distinct. Discovering this interface is always a surprise.

High winds can pile the warmer layers up at one end of a deep narrow loch so that in subsequent calm weather they surge back to the other end; after a gale, therefore, a thermal boundary is less obvious. Shallows usually possess no boundary, for the sun warms right to the bottom and wave action is relatively pronounced there.

I met this stratification for the first time in Loch Earn, one of the long narrow lochs filling a deep glacial valley.

Stepping over door-matted alder roots on the south shore, I pressed through obsequious mud to the pebbly edge and waded in. Water parted before me with little resistance. When I stopped, it stopped. When I ceased splashing with my arms the spray fell at once, and silently. I pushed off and swam for some distance along the shore at a slow crawl to warm myself up, for I had no wet-suit that day.

I soon became aware of a curious tingling in the fingers of each hand as the arm drove beneath me, disappearing whenever the stroke finished. Finger-tips became numb, despite the warmth of the rest of my body. Slowing to investigate this sensation, I allowed myself to fall into the vertical; an immediate chilling below waist-level told me the cause. The boundary

75

between warm and cold layers occurred just at arm's depth, so that at each stroke my fingers—and only my fingers—stroked the chilly mass of the loch. I had been swimming on the water's warm skin.

Diving confirmed this emphatically; but once I became accustomed to bursting the cold barrier the shock was pleasant. Sudden cold water, however, ushered me into a new world. This deep water was much sterner than occasional views from the sunlit ceiling had suggested. Although each has its own character, fresh-water lochs fall into recognizable categories. Loch Earn is one of the deep trenches. Plunging screes serve as its banks. I dived repeatedly, following the steep chute of fragments down to the limit of light—and after twenty feet or so night closes in—and saw no end to those accelerating slopes. Among the pieces of rock eels lay solitary and plump as slugs, or undulated lazily to shadow. There were no plants; only the pebbles at the edge had proffered a few knots of water moss. This ascetic diet underwater corresponded to the gauntness of surface decoration —walls of great hills, a roof of trailing cloud and, as some concession, a trimming of sombre late-summer trees.

Approaching a shallower bay I saw the slopes ease off, and could follow them down to where the stones ceased and a mud bed, tilting steeply, ran in towards the central darkness. Again there were eels, and the prints of their bellies on the mud. Leaving this emptiness I followed the bed up towards the shore, encountering at first odd stems, immensely tall and thin, which disappeared above me, and then a whole plantation of translucent threads stretching ten feet or more to the sun and air, where they relaxed into floating straps of leaves. The mud was rich, large solitary bubbles emerging from it here and there and ruffling towards the surface with the sodden dignity of jellyfish. As the water became shallower—and notably warmer all of a sudden—these pondweed stems gave place to olive-green thickets of *Nitella*, tufts of quillwort or milfoil, and merged into an endless bristle forest of rushes amongst which it was tiresome to stray. Tiresome because these lochs offer space and silence and vast unlit solitudes of a quality not found elsewhere, whereas this weed-strung pettifogging can be indulged in any casual depression.

I have swum in several of these great fresh-water lochs, Loch Ness with its 754 feet and Loch Morar, at 1,077 feet deeper than some fifty miles of the sea beyond. The stillness of such waters is memorable. Moving into it is like entering some high Norwegian corrie at nightfall, so huge and simple are the fathomless shadows closing down. One sinks, a mote in a fading sunbeam.

To explore such places for docketed information requires an aqualung and a powerful torch, but the occasional surface diver who ventures among them, even though he only dips gnat-like at their depth, learns much to his good. These cupped recesses, in wait from ice age to ice age, echo in the mind like the comparable bulk of solitary mountains, affirming a strength beyond the interplay of darkness and thin light.

Because you are, when underwater, so much more detached an observer than among mountains, so much more powerful is the impression you receive. These strange dispositions of the environment possess some disturbing significance for the human mind; and where, as in this instance, the body itself sinks apart, lit in the long evening beams, the unique isolation of man adds its own expectancy and unease.

When a similar state of mind is brought on by religious meditation or by great works of art, some relief is gained by playing the intellect around ritual or logic, orchestration or prosody; and so here in these hung solitudes you may measure back the lacustrine cycles to glacial and preglacial epochs, to the mud and rubble and ceaseless labour of mountain-building, and use your geology and physics as stylistic ornamentations. But however you treat such matters the essence is incommunicable and I merely affirm its very real existence in these waters.

I have made much of the 'play of darkness and thin light', but little of the water itself; for the water in these lochs is without character, being only a vehicle for the light, diluting and leading it into the blackness beneath. Far down, one is not aware of a surface nor sees shape or texture; one rests above contours invisible but whose mouldings are perceived by senses hitherto unused. Water appears unnecessary and therefore absent, during this cognition.

Such is the contrast between these monastic depths and the rich mysteries of the sea, whose panoply is either continually unfolding or blatantly imminent. I need not labour such differences, nor compare them with the restless incantation of rivers. My purpose is only to draw attention to the remarkable variety offered by an aquatic environment, beneath the surface of the water and—more relevantly—of the mind.

If we leave the sombre centres of these deep lochs and travel along their shores we meet, as I did at Loch Earn, various incidents such as shallow bays, and scoops in the scree bed where burns and small rivers come in. The scoops are banked with outwash fans of debris brought down perhaps when the last ice melted, and textures change rapidly as one moves over them—from silt to sand and gravel, to scattered pebbles, slaty shales or large tumbled boulders; then back again to scree. Above this delicately shifting monotony fish appear and vanish, colourless and incidental. As you proceed, veils are lifted before you, and lowered again discreetly behind.

A loch still more stark is Loch Ericht, a trench grim and treeless among the rain-swept mountains of Ben Alder. Perhaps on grey days, with winds streaming mist over the hills and raking the water to small silent curds, such a loch offers most to the connoisseur, habitué, addict, disciple or call him what you will.

Beneath the ruffled surface, light rattles a short way down among boulders and then vanishes. The water is a pure medium, without taste or feel. In a wet-suit one can drift for hours on the surface, thin rain and spray driving on the face, among subdued lapping of water and travelling gathers of wind. Above and below, wrapped in equal obscurity, huge shapes form and re-form, hesitantly ponderous; the unseen sun proceeds; and you rotate slowly from shore to shore. Compared with this, a summer's day lazing on a hill-top is fidgety, all scratching and distraction. To float Loch Ericht in the drizzle is to approach nearer the great harmony. You may prefer the one to the other, but both should be experienced.

Large shallow lochs are rare in highland country. One fine example was Loch Morlich, whose loss has already been deplored. Others tend towards reediness or eutrophic turbidity, but I remember one calm evening typical of the better places, spent in Loch Dughaill after a day on the hills. This is a shallow stony loch trimmed along one side with the massed rhododendrons of Achnashellach. The shores offered enticing labyrinths of stems and abrupt pebbly shelves, and their slopes were already softened by the approaching dusk. From the surface, across small fringed waves, one saw long black shadows of encircling hills and, on the nearer shore, rhododendrons gleaming among their pines. These lochs are best perhaps for relaxation after climbing. They are simple beneath and candid above, set among familiar mountains and deriving their character from this landscape. The water is pure and good to drink; after a hot day, to drift with mouth open, drinking and not drinking, allowing the soft liquid, mild as air, to wash away rock dust and heather pollen, is a reasonable approximation to bliss.

The water of Loch Dughaill that evening felt so warm and snug that I dallied long before turning towards the orange glow of the tent where my companion was cooking supper. Too long, for the sun had gone down and the midges had come out. Immediately on landing I was assailed by these fiends, the greatest curse of an evening swimmer in the Highlands. If swimming washes anything off the skin, it must be the repellent, not attractant, properties. A freshly emerged swimmer, tender and helpless as an exposed hermit crab, is immediately recognized and seized. To assist them, the wind falls. The few minutes between towelling and buttoning up are torment; the dusk is crawling with tiny feet and wings, white skin is freckled with their multitudes. That evening, because of the time spent afloat, I was shivering badly—though not cold—and shivering delayed the essential buttoning-up; so I was well bitten before I could enter the tent. My friend remained unsympathetic—he had been forced to cook and wait. I continued to shiver and beat the air, and spilt soup over him and his groundsheet.

Low-country lochs and lakes possess more nutrients in their water and overlie fertile muds. Those I have visited, in Scotland or abroad, lacked clarity of water and any deep starkness, but compensated for this to some extent by their cosier mysteries of cloudy vision and tangled weed. The south end of Loch Lomond, so distinct from the cloistered depths of its northern trench, runs much to sunlit mud-shallows such as I described in the bays of Loch Earn, but the Lake of Menteith or the string of smaller lochs running westward from Dunkeld below the Highland Boundary Fault display these attractions in all their dubious purity.

Entry is usually through a quag of mud, straddled with cow-pats. The turmoil pulses with insect life; water beetles and larvae of all sorts flee from your wallowing fins. Lips firmly shut, you pump through this soup and once clear of the reeds you slip away from earthy engulfment, miraculously cleansed; behind you, in disappointed clouds, writhe your cast-off sins.

The water in these lochs always seemed warm—possibly it always is in the summer, the only season I have visited them. Down in its milky recesses, threaded with strings of stems, drift and jerk shoals of small perch, their stiff red fins theatrical in the general abdication of colour. Following the mud as it shelves out deeper, one loses the surface as a living film; in its place overhead is a vague effulgence through which eventually the air might be reached. Light is everywhere, diffused and indecisive, only recovering itself sufficiently to indicate shape and texture of pondweed stalks, furred with *Vorticella*, when they are within inches of your eyes. At the bottom, pulled up suddenly, it does rather better and points out clearly a few square yards of mud, similarly furred, before wandering away to browse among the surrounding acres that lie stretched here twenty, thirty and rarely—plunged in a deeper, quite formless haze—fifty feet down. Cans and bottles, steeped in sediment, lie about where they fell, or where thrown, from anglers' boats of the past thirty years;

older ones must surely have sunk from sight. Brittle, yellowly translucent stems rise from the gentle floor, losing themselves in the brighter mist above or in the surrounding obscurity. Writhing like hooked snakes on the mud are eels; when approached and almost touched they whip themselves out of reach and sight, their wake of powdery tilth settling slowly. Following such traces, you can track them through this bizarre labyrinth of macaroni stalks until you come suddenly on their small bright eye regarding you; then away they go once more, and you leave them to their fairy-tale forest.

It is restful down below, but when you tire of unreal milky wanderings you can rise to the surface and laze there in the common sun, drifting with an occasional breeze towards bending reed-beds or persuading apart floating pondweed or lily leaves so that you may pass to browner, cobwebby, shadows beneath the alders. Pike must be active below and must often have eyed me through the swaddling haze, but I have only seen them clearly once or twice. They were small ones, a foot or so in length, sliding out of sight, their vertical bands and horizontal jaws setting them well apart from the innocent bravado of perch and the gulped meanderings of the various mud-clouded bottom-feeders who otherwise formed my company. Despite chilling tales of dog-devouring pike I never felt apprehension; the vague cotton-wool water enwrapped nothing unpleasant, in that summer sun. Families of duck drifted safely enough.

Stalking these fowl provided a diversion. If one floated motionless, it was possible to approach within a few yards of them, though they grew silent and suspicious; but any attempt to come up under them and watch from below feathery bellies and working feet was always a failure. Long before you could see them through the lightening fog, they had seen, heard or felt you and risen flapping, and you broke surface to find them, trailing water and complaining loudly, choosing another settling place a long way off.

Aimless and pleasant, but hardly challenging physically or mentally, were the sunny afternoons spent in such places.

Descending the scale to small ponds in such low-country areas, though welcome as a change, proved even less exciting. Lacking the purposiveness of the most flaccid stream, their water served as a dim vehicle for algae or stems or leaves or suchlike lip-clogging impedimenta, and any movement at all stirred up centuries of queasy sediment; its bubbling flatulence protested in my wake. And there was endless argument with surrounding pondweeds who had been there before me and intended to remain after I had gone. It was best to forget movement and accept the bell-jar, peer like a nineteenth-century naturalist at the beaded beetles passing by on the other side of your glass, the jerking water-boatmen, the caddis-fly larvae trundling their plastered kennels, the clouds of *Daphnia* and baggage-laden *Cyclops*, at tiny scufflings in the mud—*Asellus*, *Ranatra*, *Tubifex* and the bloodworms—or at the patiently climbing, swivelling, snails or, giving up, to lie hippopotamus-like on the surface and watch gnats and mayflies dance and counter-dance, exchanging their hereditary messages against the failing sun.

Whereas even the smallest pond possesses the established dignity of permanent water and its accredited inhabitants, areas of flooded ground are of interest below only for exactly what they are, accidents. Beneath the surface one encounters posts and stone dykes fixed and astonished among suspended debris; bushes project out of turbidity, refugees still clutching a few leaves, and touching one with the same incredulous gesture. The atmosphere resembles that of a recently sunk ship, where resentment stares from brass and mahogany about to be auctioned to the seaweeds. But whereas in a wreck the unreality will fade slowly, like memories of the light, under extinguishing layers of barnacle and wrack, here you know it will vanish as soon as the floods recede, when dykes and bushes emerge and the grass comes out dank and flat under an apologetic sun.

Meanwhile, to paw oneself along through the confusion (it is rarely deep enough to swim), clutching stobs, fence wire and tussocks, over buried clover and white drowned worms, is to realize the difference of a true waterscape from a landscape simply flooded. One's dissatisfaction with mere water over land enhances the subtlety of the crudest pond. To glide out from such flooded areas into the clasp of permanent water is to come home again, however irritating may be the welcoming clutter of rushes or the unexpectedly elongating pond-weed.

For small waters of full satisfaction we must go back to the hills, to the moorland tarns of England, the high *llynau* of Wales or the highland *dubh-lochan*. Set stark among rocks or heather, from a dozen to several hundred feet across, they are black in depth but silver in their sheeting, and sensitive to every shiver of wind. An island or two, carrying birch or willow scrub or preferably just coarse deer-grass, breaks the silver. Simply that, the endless sky above and the brown haunches of hills around and below them. Below them, for these lochans give the impression of being lifted up, like offerings of pure water, high to the clouds; they are of a strangely rarefied simplicity.

As you enter them, the same peat over which you walked, up which you walked, to reach them, continues under your feet, but now even less solidly; so you lie down and float out from the edge rather than step in. The only life about the surface, apart from successive thrills of breeze, moves as some lean skating insect or an occasional blown wisp of gnats. There is no vegetation beyond a fist or two of thin submerged turf. Beneath, the amber water stretches in subdued acid clarity, smoothing the peat, disappearing to stalked darkness. Small black invisible trout dart before you.

To dive through these refined solitudes, your flesh gold and bronze in the peat water, is once more to unwind the calendars; to be conscious of the slow recurrence and accumulation of the sedge, the succession of suns and floods and movements of the earth, of elevations and prostrations, of all the elemental rituals which must have moulded untold generations of hut life and spear life among such hills and waters while the ice-caps pondered, moving down, moving back. Irresistibly, these great patterns, implicit in the surrounding forms and colours, chaste but rich, immense with promise, break through his imposed complexities to the swimmer on these remote lochans.

So, resting on the sedge island, you watch this long summer evening stretch to the reach of hills, lying half on land and half in water, on an island held high to a drowning sun. The lemon sky out west is barred with black; winds are shivering purple across the water. The cry of some bird, probably a red-throated diver, arches over the dusk and disappears behind you: what other echoes are buried here, centuries under the stems and peat? Bronze rings and amulets, perhaps, or pottery, or the flattened embers of a hearth; or perhaps nothing through the folded, laid-away seasons but a trickle of small bones and beetle shells, all the way down to the glacial mud.

The wind grows colder. Your surface ruffles as the night prepares. It is, no doubt, time to sink back into the *dubh-lochan* and, moving the black wave before you, reach the shore and the track for home; before complete darkness wells up from the glens below. Already stars are shining in the invisible water.

# 8

## *About photography in the water*

For many years I had climbed and wandered the hills in all weathers, winter and summer, without a camera and never felt its loss. If occasionally at some especially remarkable sight—as on the great snow-bound upper plateau of Dalnacardoch when the crystal surface was blown for miles in a knee-high weaving iridescence—if then I had wished I could record the scene on a photograph, I always had the comfort that many friends were expert photographers who had already captured the essence of such events on their transparencies (transparencies being necessary for, unlike prints, they burn with the outdoor light); I could always borrow these slides to refresh myself and instruct the unbelieving.

I was personally reluctant to use a camera because it frequently became an end in itself. So often great scenes of natural beauty and brutality were stalked and captured simply as trophies of a photographer's ego. I thought I might be trapped like this at the second-hand and second-rate, and see corrie and buttress and snow cornice only as a function of exposure or focal length or the degree of stamping on a lecture-hall floor. Also, I had already lost so much; so many wonderful things had gone unrecorded. Why begin late, in the days of anticlimax?

My inhibitions were removed by the imminence of trips to distant parts of the world, which might not recur; and by the appearance of a young family, which would certainly not. As a result I now possess many hundreds—whisper it, even thousands—of visual records. Taking them did not lessen my enjoyment at the time, and has undoubtedly added to it since.

These slides, in fact, allow one another 'double vision'. For instance, at a warm dusk in summer, when moths dance

85

above the relaxed and moistily fragrant heads of birches, switch on the projector and show yourself those birch-tops six months previously, set them out stark on a screen, blinding white under a grey sky, bent and breaking under an intolerable crown of frozen snow, so that the agony of those slowly-gyrating candelabras, the splinter and crack of collapsing branches, the pungency of liberated birch juice, flood back into the memory; and then walk to the window and see their present decorous summer flirtation.

So, naturally, when I had time to step back from the first fascinations of underwater swimming, I began to think of photographing these waterscapes which were even less accessible than mountains to other people or myself when old or ill. If carrying a camera above water had done no harm, surely it would not distract me beneath it. But I faced other, purely technical, difficulties if I tried to take photographs under the surface. For their solution I had to wait several years, until suitable instruments and materials appeared on the market. And all this time unrepeatable sights were slipping past my eyes, rubbed out each evening by the towel.

One difficulty concerned the type of film. As I wished my picture to be as little of an artefact as possible I required colour film. Photography in black and white would give starkness and mystery and by 'modification' during development and printing it might yield very pleasing effects, but it could not reproduce even approximately the visual scene, in which colour is all-important. I needed to reproduce that scene, so that it could recreate my own underwater experience and at least suggest its appearance to others; from the imperfect but reasonably objective reproduction they could form their own idea of the reality. However, colour films need more light than black-and-white ones, and not until the advent of High-Speed Ektachrome could they be used even in my first thirty feet of water. I might have resorted to artificial light; but the neatest flash equipment is impossibly cumbrous for a single free swimmer.

Certainly, a free swimmer who wishes to take photographs is at a disadvantage when compared with an aqualung diver.

Already carrying gas cylinders, the diver finds a bulky camera and flash extension no great hardship; he never seeks rough shallow places where they could embarrass him. Down below he can slowly prowl the darkness and stalk his pictures in comfort; he has time to arrange his lighting and use patient stationary companions as lay figures or as candlesticks. Magnificent photographs and motion pictures are the result.

Driven repeatedly to capture something of the different shallower world that I knew, I attempted to use camera equipment designed for such deep divers. Let me describe one instance.

It seemed that the only way to keep a camera dry underwater was to clamp it in a box. Though curiously unskilful, I had tried to construct plastic boxes and had screwed a terrified (and cheap) camera down into them. Always they leaked, even if the design incorporated a bicycle tyre valve so you could pressurize them; the technique of pumping was difficult, too high a pressure above the surface being too low beneath, so that it seemed a bicycle pump, too, or a balloon, had to be carried with you below. Few of my contrivances ever got beyond the flooded bathroom, and the unfortunate camera scarcely ever beyond a drying fire. However, one day there appeared in a local shop a genuine underwater camera case which would fit my (good) camera and which—to judge from its price—was well enough made. Its type had been used successfully beneath various exotic seas. I was permitted to borrow it on trial. It was based on the simplest (and shortest lived) of my attempted designs, being fundamentally a large face mask bottomed to hold the camera and finished off behind in flexible rubber, with finger inserts so that controls could be operated through the rubber from outside. It had two large grip handles, one for each hand, stability fins and depth compensator, and was remarkably heavy; all this promised non-buoyancy and ease of handling.

I took it, my camera within, to a near-by mountain river on a fine summer afternoon. The water was golden-clear, the rocky bed spangled with sun. It would be a perfect day for pictures. I had the high-speed film, and carried an exposure meter in a simple transparent box. I knelt down and pushed the meter about under the surface, noting the deflection. I adjusted the camera accordingly and then stepped carefully into the water, holding both handles. The case, as I have remarked, was very expensive and possessed an alarmingly large front area of glass. This glass must not of course be broken or even scratched; scratches would ruin future pictures and force me to buy the contraption itself.

Gingerly avoiding the hitherto friendly boulders, I kicked off. I discovered that my estrangement was complete. Every stone, *every* stone, was now my enemy, bent on defacing that glass. Worse, the river itself became too strong for me. That huge face of glass was too much to push through the water upstream by legs alone. If I let go one hand to swim, the stability fins caught the current and twisted the other wrist; strokes with one free arm made steering almost impossible. Defeated, I fled, clutching the case before me, washed down with the current tadpole-wise.

I ducked behind a shore-boulder and in its quieter pool attempted to take my pictures. I dived, but the obstinate flat front of the case slowed the dive and its buoyancy plucked me away from the bottom as soon as I reached there. If in desperation I wedged myself against one bottom rock I was sure to fetch that glass a horrifying, silent, blow against another one. I had lost all companionship with the water; I was a mere exasperated slave to equipment clearly not designed for such places. The thing was useless to me. I left it—concealed, for it was expensive—on the bank and enjoyed the rest of the afternoon free once again.

I remembered that lesson well. If I were to carry a camera underwater it must be in every way as unobtrusive and easy to use as the one I carried on the hill. It was strictly to be a means. I admired a dedicated craftsman like Robert M. Adam, who clambered unwearyingly over forty years of scree with his quarter—or was it half or even full—plate instrument, lenses, cases, mahogany tripod and bundles of strapped mahogany legs, but I was not going to follow him like that beneath the surface. I had therefore to wait. When my friends shook their heads before descriptions of the underwater from either myself or other initiates, I had to repeat uselessly, 'But if only you could *see* it....'

My waiting was over when I discovered a well-known firm selling off—'selling off', mind you—a remarkable instrument. This, as its simple clarity of construction suggested, was French and designed, I believe, by Cousteau's group. An almost identical model with a possibly better lens is now available from Nikon at a high price. This camera was essentially a normal small 35 mm. model built to be waterproof. It consisted of three aluminium alloy parts: body; film transport which dropped into it; and lens, which pushed into the body and locked all three together. Two O-rings sealed the complete assembly. Capable of withstanding great pressure, corrosion-proof (even internal parts being of alloy in case of leakage), it was made for my purpose. The lens was of wide angle (for refraction of light under water reduces the effective angle of a lens) and protected by a small porthole of tough glass, itself guarded by a plastic cap. To simplify waterproofing and assist numbed fingers, all controls were rotary. The viewfinder could be held against the face mask. The whole camera was slung on a plastic strap, to be worn round the neck and fogotten about.

I have found its lens satisfactory and out of water it serves as a useful wide-angle camera. It is dustproof, naturally, and its contempt for accidents of mud, snow or rain allows one to leave it exposed on mountains, in canoes or other places where alarmed strangers remind you that your camera will be ruined. Though used by now to its imperturbability, I had anxious moments at the beginning. Even 'sold off' it was expensive enough and every reflex fought against me as I lowered it, lip-biting, into a bucket of water for the first time. One does not do that sort of thing with a camera.

Has it changed my approach to swimming? No, I think not; certainly not now I have a hundred or so reasonable underwater slides. While collecting the first dozen I admit I swam only for pictures; but then I was assuaging a hunger from years of abstention. I am easy again now.

But this kind of photography is not simple, and when one has found something to photograph then technique takes precedence over all. It is not a matter, as on the hill or in the garden, of seeing a possible picture, pausing, estimating the exposure (or swiftly checking with a meter), focusing, pressing, and moving on. And delays tiresome enough in such places—as waiting for a cloud to pass, or petals to stop shaking in the breeze, or one's companion to start climbing to the left—are appallingly magnified underwater. Let me re-enact my first day with this new camera.

I went, as before, to the near-by river. Morning sunlight scrubbed the rocks and water crystal-fresh. It was again a perfect day for photography; but this time I felt more confident.

I left the camera, at first, on the bank and dived with the exposure meter in one hand, pushing it at various angles in and out of shadow, up to the surface or down to the dappled bed. I hoped to memorise the required exposure for each position, so that at least I should have only the camera to contend with when I came to take the photographs. Because it is impossible to keep a camera steady underwater the maximum time of exposure cannot be above $1/100$ second in running water and rarely more even away from the nudge of current; one need therefore only bother about the stops. So much less to learn. I found judging light to be reasonably easy, provided I went one stop below my most pessimistic estimate; only over sunlit white sand—the equivalent of snow—has this led to over-exposure. Sunlight is essential; without its brisk whip, subtleties retire behind a gloom of damp wool only too evocative of the common conception of underwater scenes—a conception probably strengthed by looking at *prints* of colour or monochrome (as unfortunately in this very book) instead of colour *transparencies*. Prints are always muffled; transparencies sparkle.

I laid the meter on the bank, slipped the camera strap around my neck and swam out again. There was little constraint. The camera hung down freely in front of my chest and I could swim any stroke without danger of loss or entanglement or any noticeable extra friction, upstream and down-stream. I could dive holding it in both hands, poised for firing. I automatically clasped it as I pawed my way among rocks or when somersaulting; otherwise I had no worries about movement. The camera appeared ideal. Would I be competent to use it?

Now one result of looking through a mask underwater is to see everything one-third larger and nearer than it is, and consequently to underestimate distances; when one extends a huge arm to a near-by object, it falls short. The practical inconvenience is negligible; experience allows your own adjustment to be made automatically. But—and here is the snag—the encased camera must be focused for the real distance, not the apparent one. Back-tracking over my correction reflexes on the first few attempts made me think hard. Fortunately on this camera the depth of field and distance scales are coupled to the aperture control, all being visible through portholes; but the novelty of turning knobs and watching figures, and thinking about them, was strange underwater.

I was not wholly underwater; for these practice fiddlings I had wedged myself between two rocks at the banks, with snorkel above the surface. Even so, I must have spent ten minutes before pressing the trigger. It was almost impossible to keep jammed still in the swirling water. Hands shook, the viewfinder rattled against the glass of my mask, and I was certain that the large stone composing the foreground of my first waterscape—which had to be in focus—was really two, not three, metres away. The picture taken, I floated limply out of the rocks, and noticed how cold I was despite the summer water. As I mentioned earlier, the chilling inevitable when I had to lie in wait for subjects or for the right conditions forced me into a wet-suit; but this first day I wore only trunks, and suffered accordingly.

Once warmed again, I dived and searched for fish. Trout were certainly on the first day's menu. A striking group of them hung in the sun, poised behind a boulder. Attempting to frame it, I wriggled into a heap of pebbles on the bottom, knees clasping granite puddings tightly; but before I could

91

D

set sights the heap parted and I rose, puddings rolling free. Again and again I drove down and grabbed boulders, but they shifted, weightless in the water. Still the trout remained, bright in the sun. At last I jammed myself, knees and thighs below a heavy slab; I could just fight upwards, armless, against the current and raise my shoulder high enough to bring the fish into the viewfinder when—they were no longer there. Frantic scrapings brought me round to face downstream, still jammed, and I saw the same trout—or others—slowly moving across a bright background. Wonderful; but I had to change the exposure. I lowered the camera, worked out figures, twisted knobs, raised the camera: but the sun had gone in, and the fish were limp rags against a dirty blanket. I waited patiently until the cloud should pass, praying that the fish would either stop where they were or return across the gap; but something was nagging me persistently, and when my knees began to slip out from beneath the table I realized why —I needed to breathe. . . . So I pushed and scraped out, kicked to the surface and gasped in that last complication. Needless to say, the sun was now pouring forth unclouded. And, equally superfluous to note, when I had sworn and gone down under again—having first of all to find that slab—the trout had moved elsewhere.

All in all, the excitements of that day were well balanced by the frustrations, and I emerged at the end exhausted. The old rhythm had gone. I was no longer easy in the water but fighting, plotting against it, jerkily calculating amidst its immaculate abundance. Still, I had dragged out a few trophies. Of the twenty photographs risked, nine turned out too dark to see through, six were adequate, three were excellent, and two had been taken with the lens cap left on. . . .

Subsequently my skill increased. I found it was best to take fish pictures on the move, swimming up to and past them, swinging the camera like a shotgun and firing just before contact with the sights; that is, provided I had correctly forecast conditions of light, distance and movement and had set the relevant controls. Still-lifes were best taken after much selection of stances, the finest viewpoint not often offering a suitable anchorage. As the strangeness subsided, so did the trembling tension. And once I had a few reasonable slides safely docketed, the camera was slung on only in case I swam across something interesting; the correct priorities had been restored.

I found that fair likenesses could be reproduced on film of the rockier places, of weed groves and laminarian forests, though in deep water plenty of white sand was needed to set off the dark background. The most dramatic effects were against the sun, its light pulsing through the purple and gold of the kelp; in murkier waters or in rivers where grains of mica are always dancing by, dots of reflected light freckle the foreground if the sun is faced too squarely. A human figure was useful for scale, but not always welcome: it seemed to obtrude.

This jarring can arise from unsuitable colour or texture of costume. Patterns eye-catching on the beach were stripped underwater to the basic tawdriness of their designs, and the useful woollen sweaters, though less offensive in this respect, clogged any perception of rhythm. Moreover, the swimmer had to be skilled. Photographed from below a poor swimmer cannot disguise his incompetence. Frozen in struggle, his limbs protrude at crooked angles, his fingers are splayed in tetany: he clashes abominably with the aquatic assurance of his surroundings. Perhaps a good swimmer, demurely costumed, sun-bronzed so that pale flesh does not exude from the screen and facing ahead to keep the focus on the scene itself, makes the best lay figure; rubber suits, although of ideal texture, sometimes flaunt gaudy yellow seam stripes which are difficult to dispose of. Some of the most dramatic effects have been taken backwards, of my own fins breaking the surface at the beginning of a dive, or of the stream of bubbles rattling past the muscled neoprene as it vanishes downward. But generally I find the atmosphere familiar to a journeying swimmer is best reproduced by omitting the distractions of a human figure.

Of course there are more contrived pictures possible, where people do appear, if only partially: such as the feet and lower parts of pimply legged paddlers and waders or the behinds and clutched hands of small children—but there we enter parody. A swimming dog also appears ludicrous from below, especially if it is of a breed—such as a Labrador retriever—usually careful when on land to maintain at least a sheepish form of dignity; splayed paws and hairy legs jerk uncertainly, with tail—bedraggled and apologetic—venturing below at erratic intervals. Amusing, too, the view up to a rowing boat, its complacent brown belly keeled like a slug, with two enquiring oar blades glancing down every now and again; and with perhaps a vague detached hand, escorted by an ecto-plasm of bubbles, appearing beside it.

Boats tethered in harbours are favourite subjects of terrest-rial photographers. When taken from underwater they fall into equally pleasing designs. Their hulls float airships against a silvery-green sky, nosing together in groups, each rising like a kite from the long surge of its anchor rope; small moons of buoys punctuate the composition, often stitched together by loops of cable. When the water is sunny and the hulls—as of small racing yachts—brightly coloured, the buoys yellow or orange, then the effect is remarkably gay, especially if by contrast the great black green-fluffed masonry of a jetty climbs grimly past them to the surface.

I need not detail the pictures of plants and animals possible under water; the subjects are obvious, in every text-book, and patience will ensure that you surprise them at the correct conjunction of light, calm and clarity for success. Yet failures are often as memorable as the rarer triumphs. The one I am least likely to forget concerned a first attempt to photograph salmon.

The nearest water at the time was a stretch of 'fair Deveronside' above Turriff in the north-east of Scotland, where the hills above Strathbogie give way to the rich flats of Buchan. Fish were reported to be plentiful but not obvious, and I was encouraged by anglers, who had fruitlessly paced their beats, to go in and report where they were lying. I bumped across several fields by Land-Rover, squeezed through a hedge and finally slid down the steep brambly bank at a spot I was assured a likely one. I felt embarrassed, not merely by the presence of round-eyed and hopeful fishermen, but because I happened to be wearing a new weight-belt for the first time and I was sure it would be too heavy. It needed to be weighty enough to keep me steady in a powerful current, but this river was quite unknown to me and the lead I carried would have been more than adequate even in salt water. Clumsily I lowered myself off the bank, leaves and grass caught up in my buckle and camera, snorkel twanging through the willow branches.

The water flew past, silent and working agitatedly on the surface. There had been rain up in the hills. It looked very black. Silent fast rivers are disturbing. I thought of the dour Don's rejoinder to the effervescent Dee:

> For ae man ye droon
> I droon twa.

Feet finding no bottom, I let go and kicked out into midstream. I could just make way against the current, but at great effort; the inertia of my lead made me reluctant as a Rhine barge. Only the thought of great smooth bodies below —and the popping eyes above—kept me in. It was obviously useless for photography; under the surface there was nothing but a thick sepia fog, blackening fearsomely below. I would be able to see just enough for bare safety.

I swam upstream a good way, then dived. As in all such fogs, I carried my own daylight down to the pebbled bottom, which was long in revealing itself. Once there, I clutched a jag of rock. Rocks were disconcertingly evident in such a comparatively lowland river, lunging up sphinx-like around me and grumbling away to obscurity. Suddenly I saw a white flash above them, then another, and knew the salmon were about: but quite impossible to photograph. They appeared and vanished into the yellow mist like warships veering wildly on night manoeuvres; in the gloom they seemed enormous, quite eight or ten feet long. As I foresaw difficulty in returning I did not linger, and this was just as well.

I pushed off, despite the lead's reluctance, from the riverbed and naturally at right angles to it. Unfortunately this bed was not flat; it sloped steeply beneath one bank. Instead of breaking the surface, I found myself meeting through the brown fuzz—equally lit now above, below and on all sides —a wall of rock, unpleasantly broken and moving rapidly past me upstream. I realized that this was the undercut bank, gouged by the same current that was bundling me along beneath it. With one hand guarding the camera and the other fending off the malevolent thrust of river I placed both feet on this rock wall and propelled myself backwards into the body of the stream. Then when I judged I had cleared the overhang I drove upwards, head shielded, in the direction of bubbles—for in such a brown-out one blows bubbles as guides, much as one throws snowballs ahead when caught in mist on a featureless winter slope (though of course one must allow for the current carrying them to a great extent downstream as well). My emergence was more thankful than stylish, but its sputterings escaped the fishermen who were still watching, still wide-eyed, the spot far upstream—very far, it seemed—where I had originally disappeared. Consequently I had time to restore my oxygen levels before nonchalantly bellowing—if one can ever bellow with nonchalance—my news of their fish.

The place had great interest once its tricks were known, and even afforded a few photographs. The evil sepia fog and truculent rocks composed an agreeably spine-chilling picture, and the pebbly bottom abounded in eels, which slithered ghoulishly from slab to slab, long rats among sepulchres. As a final offering of this nature the river yielded me, down in one unpleasantly gouged-out pot, a large dead salmon, glowing white through the soup. As I crawled nearer to it, a black eel-head appeared from within the corpse and gestured its annoyance; then it withdrew. Twice this was repeated, before my breath ran out and before I could begin to set the camera. Every upward journey, of course, carried me downstream many yards, and returning to that given spot on the invisible river bed was exhaustingly difficult. Each time, just as my breath and patience were ended, there gleaming pallidly would be the salmon, and I had to leave it again. . . . Eventually I did photograph the body but naturally it was expecting too much of this day to hope the eel's head remained outside while I released the trigger. Twice, with exquisite perversity, the eel anticipated my forefinger. The third time I was not there.

Gathering my weights about me, I struggled to the bank, coughed out further unreliable information and, limp with relief, allowed the current to sweep me away towards Turriff, bent double, leaden-bellied and negatively buoyant. I finished at a mild bend, dragged myself up through the brambles and waited prostrate for the Land-Rover, whose twin differentials were fighting an unexpected ditch some fields upstream.

Another stimulatingly unsuccessful encounter took place not far from this last spot, off the coast of Buchan at Pennan Head. I had travelled a little along the coast below blunt-snouted cliffs, admiring the harvest bales crowning their neat-ly combed crests, and was returning at low tide exploring rock scarps which although a good way offshore were still only some fifteen feet down. The sky had turned dull and I had given up thoughts of photography, merely nosing about the weed-grown blocks piled below. The rock was pale grey and split rectilinearly, so that one curved fragment, rounded as if by wave action, stood out noticeably. Diving nearer I found its texture remarkably smooth, resembling a limb of grey marble issuing from a cavity in the rougher rock, eerie as the buried statuary in Stourhead grotto. My dive was bringing me closer to this geological curiosity, almost within touching distance, and my eye ran along its length to the dark hole: and there met another bright, single, eye.

Instantaneously I knew, tripping that malevolent glare—and knew without enquiry or reason—that I must avoid. Avoid I did, and I found myself on the surface gathering threads of rationality together. Reassembled, my observa-tions informed me that down below lay a large conger eel, and that I had narrowly missed disturbing it.

Congers have sharp teeth and an evil reputation; but I had curiosity and a camera. The challenge was offered. I returned below, to take it up. The sun, no favourable witness, had retired behind even thicker cloud, and for any hope of a pic-ture my camera setting required me to remain scarcely a metre away from suppressed rage and yearning teeth in semi-darkness fifteen feet down and a long way from shore. I shook violently, possibly from excitement, so that a satisfactory photograph appeared even less likely. The beast remained statuesque, but the cold fire behind that unwinking eye could clearly unleash an alligator fury; or so I felt as I judged the conger's body to be two metres long and thicker than my strangely tenuous thigh.

I circled for the best position, held in that unswivelling gaze. Praying that my patience would not outlast that of the eel, I let fly three shots, and backed away thankfully. They turned out poor, grossly underexposed, but by bringing the screen nearer it is possible to reconstruct that fragment of education; probably with greater effect than at the time, for the grey hulk swells hypnotically through the green Ektachrome gloom, and if the viewer is not quite reduced to the stupefaction of a cobra's victim he is at least free of the fiddling insouciance of actually taking the picture. I think that without a camera I could have explored that particular situation more rewardingly. But I was glad at the time of the excuse to beat shoreward, foaming the fresh air, safe with the precious exposures.

Automatic reaction to danger from an unexpected predator is a revealing experience, and I shall describe one later in the Mediterranean which taught me much. Although I have not stumbled across a tiger, I have been chased by a bull, threatened by a rutting stag and delivered from the occasional rockfall and avalanche, not to mention narrowly avoided pedestrian and motoring mishaps: yet none of these terrestrial emergencies has brought out the curious thrill I have felt when competent survival reflexes have operated in the apparently totally unfamiliar aquatic environment. The thrill is not experienced exclusively after the event, as a heightened survival euphoria, but coexists at the crisis with a sense of acute danger and an intellectual detachment; and a great part of it is the realization that this aquatic environment is by no means unfamiliar to our deeper responses. But, as always, one has to be easy in the water to appreciate these things; otherwise we toss confusedly between two lives

*Till human voices wake us and we drown.*

From many places on or below the surface, no transmission of experience by still photography is possible. Some situations are too vast for the tiny jaws of a cocked lens; it can nibble only a segment of the round vision. The deep lakes afford one example. The surface itself is another, where either the wave in front is in focus and drowns the horizon, or is blurred and worries the eye; and where calm water can offer only a periscopic slice of banality. Perhaps pictures of one's companions riding storm waves would be interesting, but it is difficult to keep the porthole free of spray in these conditions. Sandy shores are not satisfactory either; nor, surprisingly, are those parts of the Mediterranean I have visited, for their blue cast removes any subtlety of colour and forces one to include human figures to give scale and contrast to the often striking submarine rock formations.

But perhaps it is time we described some of these waters beyond the British Isles and left the camera as a private foible, a concession to the weaknesses of old age or a shallow eye.

*Note.* It is very difficult to reproduce on any paper prints of underwater colour transparencies taken in the subtle northern daylight, and impossible to do so satisfactorily in a book of this nature. Monochrome versions of such photographs are exceptionally lifeless. The few accompanying illustrations must therefore be regarded merely as very distant approximations to the reality; they are 'better than nothing' only if the reader realizes this. Though I am no photographic wizard, many of my underwater transparencies arouse 'stampings on the lecture-hall floor'; even a mediocre camera-wielder can produce strikingly beautiful shots with a little experience. But —they will not translate well into prints; only transparencies can bring back that wonderful living radiance.

# 9

## *About waters over the sea*

As there exist so many accounts of skin-diving in exotic waters, I intend to keep this chapter short and approach the subject a different way. I am not dealing with journeys abroad undertaken deliberately for swimming, let alone skin-diving. I shall merely record some observations which suggest how easy it is to add another dimension to your overseas travel by carrying, begging or hiring a mask, snorkel and fins. I offer no sharks, squids or wrecks. Compared with those described in narratives of sub-aquatic expeditions these waters may appear undramatic, the events trivial. I did not find them so nor, I believe, would anyone who was sympathetic to the aims of this book—nor any ordinary interested traveller.

I repeat, these trips were in no sense expeditions, never being made for the sake of swimming. Rather, when landing at any spot, however briefly, I always tried to grasp its local interpretation of our globe by climbing its nearest hills and swimming in its nearest waters; this also affords a useful background to its human society. Again, because most of my trips were by plane and for professional reasons, I had little room for extra equipment. I recall, for instance strolling on a dry glacier in overcoat and baseball sneakers with an expensive Swedish barbecue fork (later shamelessly straightened back into a gift) as an alpenstock, skiing through Finnish woods in a lounge suit and scraping the steamy piecrust of a Japanese volcano in city shoes. My aquatic apparel has been equally incongruous, though never inadequate; a piece of garden hose, for example, tied to a cane makes an excellent snorkel provided one doesn't bite—or suck—too hard.

So I shall only describe fleeting days in and out of the waters of the world, days that anyone can enjoy who has a mind to, and who treats the seas, lakes and rivers as just as worthy a part of the globe as the rather over-documented land. Let us begin with fresh water, and an episode quite uneventful but typically satisfying.

Every summer weekend Montreal empties into the surrounding Laurentians, three-tone horns in tens of thousands streaming through forest roads to ultimate dispersion. For my one weekend I jolted there in a dusty bus, being at length extricated by a friend and led along woodland tracks to his cabin. Through lush sunlight poplars and spruce thrust upwards, and leaf-hidden hammerings on all sides proclaimed the burgeoning of summer homes. The trail up the local branch-entangled summit revealed eventually other spruce-furred undulations which hazed into a blue distance buttoned with small lakes—and we were to go down and swim in the nearest one. Our descent wound through Chevrolets and Falcons stowed alongside intermittent camping sites, and the greasy weight of mask and fins, slung in a hot towel, only became bearable as the path threaded lower and the timber dipped obviously to a lake. Then the trees stopped and the glitter appeared.

Like the rest of this amenity area, the waterside alternated between assertive wilderness and trampling suburbia, forested islands and shore being scrambled with cabins and the surface of the astonishingly blue water jerking with power-boats. The noise was as deafening as the heat; but both vanished as I launched myself in, with the relief of a long-delayed commuter turning his front-door key.

The water was cloudy, but not unpleasantly so, and I threshed away from the crowded beach, dodging between the power-boats like a skilled jay-walker, and reached safety in a peaceful area among small islands. A week of international dust and discussion dissolved away to the receptive hydrozoa as I floated under a pumping sun. Round and round flew the power-boats, some whipping water skiers after them, others spinning with cheerful, purposeless intent; hydroplanes skimmed past, balanced with blondes and transistors. Behind me, island chipmunks grumbled and scratched among the cones.

I floated in bliss; and allowed eastern North America to work away.

I drowsed along the shores of islands, moving through flotillas of spruce needles, surface ears assailed by the sudden zip as a craft flew past a gap, ears underwater hearing a continuous faint and tinny resonance, rising and falling. Even when, after a perilous sprint back to the lake edge, I was drifting safe among overhanging boughs only a few metres away from their plunging circuit, I could never estimate under water how near those engines were nor from what direction they would come; the spidery complaints were not distracting down there among the mud and settled needles, but sounded as pleasantly irrelevant as the evening unwinding of cicadas in some remote Alpine valley. Surfacing to reality, therefore, required great care, and I kept strictly to the periphery, my brachiosaural emergence at one point causing panic among a waterside picnic of small children—when I at once retired beneath the surface again, closing off shrieks of rebuke and shutting down the forty-horsepower Johnsons and Mercurys to the distant murmur of *les cigales*.

Equally officious with surface craft and equally refreshing after weeks of dust was a day in Lac d'Annecy, which introduced me to the milky delights of glacier water—water which when in its rivers, blinding and drubbing, I had certainly avoided. Placid as in the Lac d'Annecy, brightly illuminated by the sun, it afforded below the surface an infinitely receding universe of eggshell green in which one's movement could scarcely be judged at all, and direction guessed at only by the slightest darkening beneath; for the suspended particles were too small to fix with the eye and they scattered the light at all angles, being virtually as bright below as above. I discovered my ears to be the best indicators of depth and often found myself, when apparently proceeding horizontally, ramming into an approaching band of eardrum-hammering water. There is neither form, sound or movement below and one's reactions, after casting about in bewilderment, resign themselves glumly to the principles of Einstein. Only the invaluable bubbles serve as guide and however disastrous it might seem to dive downwards after them to reach the surface they had to be trusted—like the compass in mist that you feel must be wrong yet dare not disobey.

Surface swimming on such lakes, fringed with villas and backed by the Alps, is of course enjoyable provided the motor-boats and duck-complacent holiday steamers are avoided, but is scarcely distinct enough to merit description here. Nor are the many bathes in Alpine pools worth recording, for they and their like come only as welcome episodes in a terrestrial day. Nor the fine lake above Kvamskogen in Norway where I hunted trout through waving hectares of watergrass and caught one—in a picture—straddled by a search-beam from the groping sun: for that was but one lake among many. Nor even that shallow rock basin high in the bare slabs near by, so welcome after broiling hours among Takvitingen's glacier and false summits; I had no equipment at all there, nor even time to put more than head and shoulders in, but, eyelashes or no eyelashes, I drank with mouth and eye clear cold draughts of flat, collected, tranquillity; then out and down the rubble and clattering gullies again.

Nor should I linger over such a well-known mountain lake as that at Flims, discreetly commercialized and thanks to its warm-spring water almost approaching the ideal aquatic park, with wooded islands, reedy inlets, bridgelets, rafts, chutes and painted boats; yet after weeks of climbing, a few circuits of those bland waters were singularly refreshing. The other occupants afforded mild interest, too, ranging from, on the surface, an elderly Swiss well out into the lake smoking imperturbably above his breast stroke an undamped cigar (with—to my awe—an inch or so of adherent ash) to bottom dwellers such as an enormous bejowled carp who repeatedly blew mud across my lens. Although this lake was not exciting underwater, the advantages in range and effort afforded by mask and fins were very obvious; yet no one else of the hundred or so swimmers was using them and apart from a few fifty-metre threshers-out-and-back and the venturesome eccentric with a cigar, all were congregated at the cloudiest and least attractive area, that nearest the entrance. Perhaps, even if all had mask and fins they would remain there, much as skiers congeal round the dullest of peel-strewn pistes while the whole mountainside invites them in vain.

Rather, I think, I should recommend the endless lonely lakes of Finland and South Sweden, that resemble those half a world away on the Canadian Shield but appear flatter and more fragilely calm among their birch and conifers, shored alternately by mud and smooth granite; always with islands of every size signalling from open stretches and always, among the closed encircling forests, water escaping with a glint through creeks and passages. These places are pre-eminently for surface swimming and, lying back, fins working silently, one notes the ever-receding wake ripple dark on the silver water or break sunlit in the shade of trees; and sees how infinitely complex are the patterns of branches and glitter that unwind soundlessly by. Islands of reeds and humped granite, islands of spruce and aspen, of birch, large islands where the roe families peer down between the pine trunks of a bald headland; backwaters and bays, spruce-drooping, heavy with resin, where surely one should see, sometime this evening, the distant, earnest head of an elk, urging its antlers from one shore to another, grunting and splashing through the dusk.

Then later, by moonlight, one can swim out in the oil-smooth darkness. One such night I moved a little way from the shore pushing before me a log, and then drifted with it out of the shadow into the open moon-sparkle. My hands rested on the bark and the log itself nosed black and square, ploughing in silver until slowly, imperceptibly, ceasing to move. Silence was intense. Water and forest and water stretched ahead to beyond the Arctic Circle, quenched in the night. Out there above, the Pole Star; lurching under my fingers, the rough scented pine. The liquid night shivered with constellations and small cracklings ran from island to island around me. My feet stirred endless black suspension. So little of this country, of this great northern quarter of the world, can be grasped from land—one has only glimpses. At night in these lakes it floats bare.

I left the log lying blocked alone in the glitter and drew soundlessly (how one can feast on the silences there!) back to the reed-patting shore.

This is canoe country, too, but a canoeist forfeits the resilience of a sudden dive to the hollowed granite below and the vast competence of its settled miles of gravel and mud; he must lack such a confident grip of this delicately undulating country where land and water connive so privately. Canoeing, you journey through these places; swimming, you are part of them. Like the landscape, you enter and leave the water continually, and without haste. The taste of the water lies silk on the tongue, pine needles dry on to damp skin, streams run from your bathing trunks across the sun-warm granite. Far indeed from Loch Ericht in the rain, but an equal identity with your surroundings. Effortless to slip again into the water, effortless to rise again on to another islet, effortless to weave below after the strings of perch, or to drift where the wavelets slop tidily among the polished boulders. Then homeward in the evening along needle-soft tracks in the aromatic woods, blaeberry and fern scraping the shins. . . . In recent years lakes have become tainted even in so civilized a country as Sweden, but Finland offers an inexhaustible amplitude of water, marred only in the north by mosquitoes and, in society, by the (to me) barbaric consummatory plunge after the *sauna*.

In winter it is fascinating to re-visit these same lakes, travelling from familiar island to island, but this time fugitive, lank and creaking on ski. Beneath its skin of snow, ice jars solid against the points of your sticks; you are locked out. You journey on, leaving, like the printed roe and elk, a wake permanent until the next blizzard.

Which should send me north, to Iceland, land of fire and ice, its waters boiled by magma or chilled by glaciers. The ordinary lakes there resemble the flatter Scottish upland lochs and the rivers, turbid and unpredictable, doze through miles of braided sands or battle Valhallas in gorges, and I never trusted myself to enter them. The springs proved the most interesting. They welled through fissures in the lava and either lay down there in the dark or collected outside in large clear pools. They could be cold or hot. I entered the cold first, but very briefly. The water in these cracks is achingly frigid to bare skin, and saw-tooth rocks, shadowed by deeper black crevasses, inhibit any movement rapid enough to warm you. Neither is a wet-suit satisfactory. The cindery lava drags silently at the neoprene; one should feel the abrasure, but does not, and mistrust begins.

The slits gape maybe two or three feet across and a hundred jagged yards long, repeating perhaps for hundreds more, and their depth to water-level may be a few feet or dozens; the water itself reaches impossibly deep down, through one constriction after another. Yet where the sunlight strikes the water, they possess a grim beauty. A glass-still blueness is framed by diamonded walls, the lava grotesquely fanged as if crystallized suddenly from a great storm. One steals among a frozen sea of rock in some perilous temporary winter. Here and there along the twisted ledges puff out blue-green algae, and in one spring beside the road at Thingvellir shining piles of coins added to the drama. All these incidents are welcome. Nothing appears paltry or incongruous in what is so evidently a lull in the earth's forging; one is grateful for any gesture, any sort of company. Sunken bottles and drowned cans, as much as the untidy towns themselves, acquire a kind of nobility set between such jaws.

But these cold springs were very cold and although I warmed up a little in a shallow lake floored with coils of ropy lava and which, to make quite clear to me the transience of everything in this land, had tilted itself very recently, only the true hot springs restored the imbalance, for they were hot indeed.

An example of these, not far from Mývatn, is much used as a washing place. It flows through two separate caves, one for men, the other for women; as is proper, the men bathe upstream. My wife having been dismissed to inferior waters by the bellow of *Nur für Herren!* (in the first foreign language to come to the alarmed occupants' mind), I entered my cave very willingly; I had driven that day through hours of desert dust.

It was, as strangely inevitable in such an apparently sparsely populated country as Iceland, crowded. I clambered down slippery rock steps past steaming bodies and undressed on a warm wet ledge. Smooth black water several feet across hastened beneath us, vanishing through a crack some six or so yards away into the ladies' pool. Although most of my fellow-bathers were naked I felt constrained by decency, having brought mask and fins and even a camera, to wear trunks. The others took no notice. Sweating and torpid, they lay around unseeing; only three of them were in the pool, two treading water with gentle sighs, the third grasping a ledge and floating half-submerged with the timeless, glazed eyes of a frog.

I entered a hot bath, hot enough to make me fear for my rubber and film. I left the camera on the side and, warily, struck out. Swimming in hot water was quite different from any previous aquatic experience, especially in such a steamy underground pot. This water insisted on itself, pawing me, fingering my throat. I had to thrust it off. The pool was deep and clear. I dived down to the bottom and gazed up telescopically at dangling legs and the undulating blob of the cave entrance. Several times I dived, even ungallantly exploring the outlet to the ladies' cave; it was fortunately too narrow for me to risk an unworthy end by jamming or from Maenadic retribution. Then I began to feel strangely tired and my heart started to pound noisily; the water tightened its grip on my throat. I bubbled upwards, blew and gasped, and limped to the side, staying by the motionless frog-like individual for some moments, then emerged and draped myself, panting, among the others. I now understood their inertia. It came not from boredom nor from good manners, but from simple hyperthermia. I was extremely hyperthermic. My eyeballs rattled in a dizzy head. Of course you shouldn't swim hard in hot water; there is no way of cooling off.

Chastened, I returned cautiously and even tried a few

snapshots from below, but although I can recognize in the result the smoothed lava pillars of our well, the concentric ledges ringing upwards to the splash of light, even distinguish a dangling leg, no one else can—or will. The film, however, did not melt. But it was more pleasant to drift about, exploring the darkness unhurriedly, emerging to bask in the coolness every few minutes. Mask and fins gave freedom of the quite intricate depths of this pool, the narrowing and openings, its submerged apses and side-chapels. I made the most of it. The first interest over, it became a pot to soak in, a washing place, nothing more. The surface was dull and the water not enjoyable in itself. Real refreshment came later, on stumbling out into the slicing light and wind; but at least I was clean— and the current ran so fast my wife was, also.

A famous open-air hot pool in Iceland is at Landmanna-laugar in the south, and we bumped and rattled there by Land-Rover through dust storms transmuted by rain into blizzards of mud. The last river before this place was half a mile wide and in spate; headlights revealed an infinity of impassable horror, so we camped beside it. Throughout the night Icelanders arrived and drove in disbelief up and down the banks, honking and flashing disconsolately. This race is not easily put off; one member waded up to the middle of his grey suit, within six feet of the shore, before concluding that his jeep and caravan might not make it, and another, less circumspect, spent the next three days recovering, dismantling, drying out and reassembling his drowned Land-Rover. However, the following morning was sunny and the whole family, strung with rope across a mud-sided mountain, made an overland route to the hot pool.

It was set in a little meadow of bright, poisonous green beneath a steaming cataract of obsidian. Before it ran the yellow river, now being vigorously crossed by various Leifur Eiríkssons. Around it rose chemical mountains of every mineral tint. The tang of sun and sulphur was in the air. The children, inured to rigours of glacial paddling, viewed the steaming ponds and their little interconnecting ditches with suspicion. It was soon dispelled. The new world announced itself underfoot, where wet cold grass changed into wet warm grass and your quaggy footsteps dislodged clouds of steam. The small creatures could leap and dance as though on a monstrous bathroom sponge; and so began their first whole day of swimming and splashing, recalled nostalgically through later years of southern temperance.

The pool was so hot that you lowered a leg into it carefully, as if testing a bath, and only gradually slid yourself in. Steam writhed around you, sulphurous vapours prickled your nose and throat. The floor was gruesome crust, scabbed with minerals, hot pulp beneath, and shifted as you trod it. The water tasted of metal. Cruising across these pools one looked down and saw bubbles of gas budding and flowering, and then fruiting to the surface; thermophilous algae drifted in clots, but the water was clear and kept so by its continual issue.

These feeding wells were either hot or cool, and could be detected not only by movement of sediment on the floor, but by the diffraction of light through their differing densities. Continuous messages of heat and chill brushed the skin and one could hook on to a current of one or the other and follow it as an invisible thread until it wandered, frayed and eventually failed near the pool's exit. Beside the hot wells the mud was scorching to feet or hands, and after a thorough basting in culinary bubbles one could float to a cold stream and drift or hover in its refreshing tremulousness; until the fire called you back. When over-cooked, it was strangely luxurious to haul half out on to warm rough rushes and orange hawkweed, and allow cool winds to smooth the shoulders; to see the bizarre red-eyed mountains beyond and watch the cold racing river, a few yards across the bog, frothing in midstream around the roof of last night's washed-away Land-Rover.

The farthest north of Iceland just fails by a few miles to make the Polar Circle. Rather self-consciously I had decided to enter the sea at this point; it seemed the next best thing to swimming off Greenland—just over there to the west—and perhaps it would be interesting. I had hoped for ice floes, but the only ones that summer were collected farther south-west in Húnaflói, as I had noted on the way up; all were stranded out in the bay except one group hard under the cliffs, and after much wading through bogs I had slid down to the shore and inspected them. Electric blue on that dull day and with small fish swarming round them, they promised fine under-water grottoes. As I would be returning that way within a week I decided to postpone the swim until then, when the weather might be brighter—besides, there would be other floes farther north. Frankly, I could not face the double journey through the bogs again that day laden with kit and weight-belt. I assumed that such huge, frozen slabs would scarcely melt in a week. My physics was faulty, for when I did return not a morsel of ice remained in the bay.

At my farthest north, off Melrakkasletta, there were no floes at all, merely a flat, black-wracked beach projecting beyond the final sputters of lava. South-westward gleamed the zebra-striped snow mountains beside Eyjafjordur. Every-thing pointed expectantly to the open, patently Arctic, north. The water was, however, apart from its geographical position, uninteresting; not even distinguished by cold. Once free of the remarkably diverse plastic flotsam of the beach (these shores collect much garbage from fishing fleets) one could appreci-ate the sour economy of an abraded volcanic coastline, and the intense loneliness of Polar waters feeling into their first land. As under-surface visibility was poor and vegetation sparse, the area offered only this unrivalled kind of horizon-gazing. Doubtless the massively bare blunt fjords of north-west Iceland would have been impressive from the surface, but I did not swim in them; off the south coast, black volcanic sands and red cindered cliffs provided a curious background to green and yellow algae, but again I did not explore them fully underwater. I judged the shallow-water scenery off Ice-land interesting rather for its strangeness of rock than of vege-tation and this strangeness was best sampled in the quiet freshwater clefts and pools I described earlier.

I found a curious local underwater form and colouring off the Norwegian coast, near Bergen. The difficulty with sea-swimming there is to find access to the water; all shores less than vertical have been pegged out by huts and cabins. Legislation has come too late. Near the town itself I did manage to enter the sea, but only at the end of a very long inlet and after much exchange of helpful introductions: from the garden of the country-dance society's building.... My wife remained ashore as a kind of hostage for courtesy and was already well out of her depth in a surrounding flood of Scando-Scottish Terpsichorean enthusiasm before I had waded more than a few yards from the well-flattened lawn.

The journey seaward took me through warm brown-brackish water, above mussel-beds being feasted on by prising bands of starfish, past wooded banks, huts and villas, under a bridge and finally, among nests of small boats, out to unquestionably seaweedy sea, colder and bobbing with round, black waves. It is always pleasant to visit boats when swimming, to pass between them, restless, stamping, lumpish, tethered like horses in a stable; always, too, with an eye to a kick from their swung stern-edges, a rope jerked out of the water in front of you, or a bony nuzzling of bows. The slapping and gurgling as wavelets echo among them is reminiscent of the sounds when you yourself slip into the water, but tauter, more resonant, less yielding, and indeed boats as seen by a swimmer appear strangely unsympathetic to the water; they float on, pass over and are tolerated by this element, but are never accepted as he is. Rubber boats, though clumsily buckling and slobbering, appear less foreign, and their flesh resembles your own. I spent much of my youth messing about with boats and in my land life never suspected this disharmony; from above, a good boat appears to fit its water perfectly. Swimming off Norway, or Scandinavia generally, one is always encountering boats; eventually one feels like a tramp caught up in a fox-hunting meet and, blown on and scrutinized from above, one is glad enough to slip over rocks into some enclosure where these mounts cannot possibly follow.

The shapes and colourings were most notable farther south, in the Lysefjord and Fusafjord area. In cold, pale-blue water glowed a variety of pastel hues, pinks, yellows, ochres, reds, all thinned to a milkiness reflected in the tenuous shapes —fringed and furred, mossed with pale algae and hydroids, and darting with small, pale fish. Through this refulgent fluff gleamed occasionally a lurid, blood-red anenome. Boulders like wads of cotton wool padded off to blanketed depths. Only the piercingly cold water kept one tightly apart from such mollycoddling.

The Baltic shores of Sweden and Finland resemble closely their freshwater lakes; the occasional seaweed is all the more surprising. Water, though, is never limpid in this diluted sea, but if flat is flaccid, with an aftertaste of salt. A hybrid scene; which is best summed up by a glimpse of a huge pike, or so it seemed, sailing off from rushes towards a deep clump of kelp-like weed, rolling its eyes—pike appear to possess this faculty more than other fish—backwards in heavy distaste. Coarser, then, with rougher shores than the inland waters and threaded by honking and more blustering vessels, the sea among the Stockholm or the Finnish archipelagos is still varied and delightful and, despite increasing pollution, among the most pleasant regions of Europe for surface swimming.

The most pleasant, in general opinion, is of course the Mediterranean, for swimming both on the surface and beneath. My first introduction to this sea was from Corsica. We had sailed there over the requisite wine-dark waves and, even though mountaineering was our main objective, no sooner had we landed and driven outside Bastia than the accumulated foreign dust of England and France became unbearable; we stopped where the sea licked the first crackle of *maquis*, tore off clothes and plunged into the open arms of a shallow bay. Among sun-bleached rock and hard aromatic leaves, among such rough heat and prickles, the velvet blue water provoked an urgent desire.

When somewhat sated, one could observe the curious blue clarity underwater, the monochromatic wash over all colours except in the shallowest places, a blueness through which rocks loomed spectrally; they carried a scattered black scrub of seaweed remarkably similar to the sparse *maquis* itself. Much of the pleasure, then and subsequently, came from the brightness and simplicity of the surface vision; on a dull day it was dead and meagre both above and below. If the West Highland waterscape had been transported there on a fine day, under such a sun its colour and luxuriance would have transformed the relatively unexciting Mediterranean scene. But let me not cavil. The water was warm—at least near the surface—and pleasingly limpid, and the blueness strange. Leaving the others, I swam well out into the bay. These first exotic waters deserved to be enjoyed alone.

From far out, floating in a shell of sunlight, I surveyed the green and brown hills, humped to their private island clouds; around me stretched the Homeric sea, bland and almost black under the enamelled sun. The water was soft to the fingers; I freckled its surface with my hands and dreamed of Troy, of all those long-bleached battles, of galleys making westward to Iberia and to the cold grey waves outside the garden wall. Amidst such reveries my eye caught sight of a white-fringed triangle breaking the surface a hundred yards or so away.

I suddenly found myself threshing shorewards. I distinctly remember the thoughts' jolting into position, one after the other as my brain struggled to regain control like an over-thrown charioteer scrambling back to his reins or a surf-rider, caught out of balance, clawing desperately forwards. The sequence ran: triangle—triangular fin—shark—sharks in warm waters—sharks in Mediterranean—swimmer lost last week off Sicily, believed taken by shark—shark here—shark swims faster than you—attracted by splashing—don't splash —stop and face it—stop—STOP. And I stopped, still with one half watching the other screw down the reflexes to a halt. I turned round, but the shape was still where it had been, still triangular; but less obviously a shark's fin. I do not know what it could have been; I left it, and moved carefully backwards, watching.

That has been my only experience of panic in the water and it was marked by the immediacy of the flight reaction, which was clearly in progress before I had grasped the reason, and by the equally perceptible grinding of this flight to a halt by the application of rational brakes. A most curious, but disturbing, event and the only time I have disagreed with the body's automatic response in the water; but I was in a strange sea not yet understood and it was a surface occurrence —happening underwater I rather think my flesh would not have risked fleeing eyeless but would have backed away and bristled all it could, in the traditional manner.

I have had no further meetings with sharks real or imagined, so I cannot claim to have proved my hypothesis. Certainly I dislike the idea of encountering a shark; even large dogfish make me reach for my knife. Perhaps the Elasmobranchs cast too long a shadow in time; genuine vertebrates—such as the conger eel of the last chapter or the seals of the next but one, or even killer whales—though less easily fooled do appear more acceptable as ocean mates.

No, there are no heroics in these pages, and as the Mediterranean has been often enough described I shall not dwell on the day-long delights of swimming there: across wide sandy bays whose yellow clarified the blue underwater to a thin acid green until you were so far out that the darkness came in again below for what seemed hours, and the pines you had left behind sank under their mountains to a blur while the ones you were approaching raised themselves ever so slowly out of the corresponding haze under the opposite hills, and your back scorched in the sun; or the deep cold dives in pale and sombre shadows among tall white rocks like drowned megaliths, depths all the colder because of the ample upper warmth. It is all very enjoyable if a little unsubtle compared with my home waters; possibly the difference between high noon in Crete and in the Hebrides—a clear simple statement, against endless queries and qualifications.

Moving farther south we can take, as a final example, the Pacific off the Hawaiian Islands. Again—these being hallowed story-telling waters—I shall offer no epic, but record them as they appeared to North Atlantic eyes during three days between planes.

I had left the pearl-farmed shores of Japan (a chapter in themselves, those underwater corrals and forcing-pens, but we have no space here) and, freed from work, intended to luxuriate at Waikiki before moving on to the States. And the obvious thing to do at Waikiki was to swim; December would make no difference there. There are vastly better places to swim in those islands than Waikiki, but I had no time to spend travelling about and this chapter is meant to illustrate how you can enjoy strange swimming as easily as walking, in the brief intervals of a flight schedule. Given time, I would have climbed Mauna Kea and swum off Kauai; as it was, I scrambled up Diamond Head and swam from Waikiki.

The 50th State is pleasantly wrapped in polythene, with much of its freshness preserved, and its inhabitants are mercifully indolent; so that arrangements slid together efficiently without haste. I landed before breakfast, checked in at a beach hotel, ate, went down among lounging palms and sand-bathers and, from a kind of windowless, unwalled West Highland store, hired mask, fins, snorkel and swimming trunks. I returned to the hotel, changed, and rejoined the hundred or so idlers on that vast lazy beach so generous with imported gold: truck-loads yearly replenish its sand.... My northern whiteness, which never would, this trip, have time to acquire the background brown, dazzled the natives to curiosity. I asked them about currents, conditions and so on; they warned me of surf at such a place, fish and spines to avoid, and enquired wonderingly of waters at 50° F. Mutually sustained, we parted, and I walked down to the high-stepping waves.

If the Mediterranean had been slightly disappointing, this water was not. After all, the whole resources of the Pacific were behind it, and the frippery building along the shore vanished under the elegant competence of palms and forested mountain, the easy strength of coast-line and sky. The air was fresh and crisp, for 74°. Probably because of the South Sea Spell, activities that would have appeared tiresomely contrived along the Mediterranean or Californian coast, such as footling about in pedal boats or being paddled, fat-bellied, out in canoes by hired and sardonic hairy men, here escaped the critical eye. Everyone, fat-bellied or not, was living without effort, carelessly and spontaneously; or so it seemed to one just released from hours and hours of pressurized Pan-Am.

The advancing waves were peppered with surf-riders, whose boards winked red, yellow and blue against the sun, and long white canoes rode in through the foam, their paddles flashing; bright-sailed catamarans wheeled far out. I chose a quiet area and waded in. The water was cool, imperceptibly warm: that rare quality of being 'just right'. It possessed a curious pale green translucence, singingly clear and primitive, quite unlike those old wine-lees, so often drained, of the Mediterranean. It was not a weary sea, nor yet a naïve one; it had the boned strength I had recognized in the North Atlantic, but also a gaiety certainly missing there. This fascinating water took me over for my three days and showed me many new things.

One of course was its fish. Unlike those in home waters or even in the Mediterranean, the fish here were immediately apparent, and flaunted themselves. I no sooner lowered my head on to the gentle water than I saw them, incredible numbers of them, flashing or cruising or nosing about, arranged tidily in those shoals we have all seen photographed and in those same brilliant slap-of-paint colours. The remarkably transparent water—not merely clear—held them in a great bowl over the golden sand; in this place there was no vegetation to compete, and colour, shape, texture and movement were all supplied by the fish, who arranged themselves in a perpetual kaleidoscope, restless and soundless, flitting into and out of curiously symmetrical patterns. The shyness or, at best, unconcern of northern fish was absent; lying on the bottom I was very soon surrounded by them, snuffing and poking, well within arm's reach. Clasping some coral, I allowed the gaudy multitudes to congregate around me: orange, crimson, azure, flour-white and fathomless black, striped, slashed or carefully divided in colour; iridescently deflecting the sun or murmurously velveted; beaked, snouted, rubber-lipped or tight-jawed; but all notably sedate and confident in demeanour, weaving and counter-weaving beside and above me so that, at times, like a thick fall of leaves, they darkened the sun.

Later I moved farther towards Diamond and Koko Heads:

and among the broken rocks and pink and orange corals, in the rusty shadows, these fish appeared less overwhelming than over plain sand. Against the smouldering background of colour they moved almost with the modesty of our northern saithe and pollack. Being so new to this area I myself felt more conspicuous and hunched tenderly white among possibly poisonous spines and prickles, watching warily for bigger fish; splendid silvery torpedoes glided farther out where the coral dropped away, in the pale, very pale, clear blueness, shivering their black tail-fins among shoal after shoal—fragmenting galaxies—of lesser fry. I did not venture after them. Inshore, the colours of corals and animals were as satisfying as those off the Western Highlands, reds, purples and oranges balancing the green and blue distance and the yellow sand, but I missed the mop-luxuriance of our vegetation. As recompense, here the light breathed a splendour unknown before and arched into immense and fearful vaultings. Offshore, great breakers thundered and dissolved, their trapped air flashing like sheet lightning through the distant rocks. Only two days old, I clung by the coral and relished the strangeness.

But of the delights of tropical reefs enough has already been written. What else did I savour off this island? The water being so lucid and the air so warm, I found the surface less tangible than elsewhere and the waves, large as they were, less material: one slipped through them with little resistance. Only near the beach did they put on obvious strength, towering and letting down their hair more meaningfully, but—with no rocks near—one could ride on to the shore with them as on a board.

Real surf-boards abounded in the sea opposite the hotels, and from down below one saw them hovering above like floating beetles; then, as they caught their wave, up and off they would go, hoisted, jerking and dipping among bubbles either out of sight or, if an upset occurred, dissolving into clouds of air, spinning edges and gesticulating limbs. One could see half a dozen at a time, and as many more being pushed along by truncated swimmers, whose legs fussed the delicate surface.

Impressive from below were the great white outriggers and catamarans; you could measure the curling wavecrests along their flanks and sense the fierceness of the abrupt stabs of paddles bursting down first one side then the other. Yet even these most seaworthy craft lay stiff on the water, only the fish and your own limbs moving in sympathy with it. There were few swimmers, and even fewer with mask and fins; but how revealing it was to see two expert spear-fishers striking out for the reefs through half a dozen or so bare-foot swimmers by the shore; these last, though competent, appeared hurried and wasteful of energy, wrapped in an irritation of bubbles, while the fishermen even on the surface sped along with minimum of movement and on their dives flitted away with marvellous economy through the parting shoals of fish.

The three days sufficed to make these waters the norm for swimming and when I had handed back my equipment and sat waiting in the tropical night by the warm fountains outside the airport, among fruitbats and huge moths, the gaunt statements of Loch Treig or Loch Earn were as remote as their improbable ice ages. Calvin's stone face had disappeared beneath the hibiscus.

Yet next day, among snow-combed red cedars in the Cascade Mountains, all I had as proof of my Pacific was a back so blistered that every ski turn was agony, and I shed skin right up to Vancouver. Even in those waters I should have worn a shirt, this time against the too-hospitable sun.

# 10
## *About touring in rivers*

It is now time to describe something of the pleasures of touring in the water; of spending a day travelling aquatically, but enjoying intervals of haul-out on skerry or shore much as a terrestrial rambler might refresh himself by plunges in the occasional pool or river. As I have already suggested, such a day of swimming is no more, and probably less, strenuous than one spent walking over the hills; though if rough water is sought, as in fast rivers or white seas, then the likeness is rather to climbing difficult rock or ice, and the commitment is correspondingly greater.

I have—as explained earlier—been chary of offering detailed advice in this book in case the reader came to regard it as a manual of instruction. These text-books abound, and provide a sound basis for elementary skin-diving or fishing, but they do treat 'touring' rather scantily. I shall therefore add here and there a few observations to fill up this deficiency, even though my own practice has not always been faithful to what I preach.

Firstly, always take a companion. Always take, also, some food such as water-proofed glucose sweets, even if you have cached ampler supplies along your route. Again, always see that someone knows of your intended route, and of your probable short cuts or landings if the weather worsens; these last are most important, for to persevere along your original route—in water or among hills—against your better judgement just because you fear commotion at the other end if you don't get there, is a common and dangerous temptation. Always take a knife. Other impediments, such as torch or whistle, could be thought of as useful, but add to frictional drag. You should be able to float easily enough for presumably, in the sea at any rate, you will be wearing a wet-suit and quick-release belt.

You should, for these long trips, invest in a hood. Hoods need to be wrenched on or off, muffle your ears and clamp your jaws (so that shifting your mouthpiece or chewing your sandwich becomes a task for both hands) but they do prevent heat loss from your after all fairly important head. With a hood the fiercest waves break harmlessly outside your port-hole and you can snuggle down to doze in the foulest weather. You lose of course much of your surface hearing, but contact noises—such as weed strings stroking your neoprene—are magnified, alarmingly so at first.

Your equipment must be sound, and examined thoroughly before and during the trip much as one checks one's ski bindings or ropes continually among high mountains. The straps of mask and fins especially should be examined for perishing or slipping; I carry a length of spare strap. Obviously loss of a fin is crippling for a solitary swimmer far out and is one of the many reasons why, for journeys of more than say twenty minutes from land in tides of average strength, at least one companion is essential, even for the experienced. I lost a fin fairly near the land, and homeward progress exactly resembled the frustrating dot-and-dash of a single-planked skier; later, at low tide, a corkscrew dive surprisingly recovered the fin. Floating ones are better, but are curiously difficult to locate, especially in rough water.

But such touring as I have in mind does not entail prolonged swimming far out from shore. These more open places are exciting to traverse or pleasant to drift in a little, but are not usually for spending one's whole day; nearer the shore, among the skerries and underwater grottoes as they unwind along the coast—that is the delectable region.

To begin with, however, we shall take a river whose banks are unquestionably close, and a fast mountain river at that; for, as we saw earlier, these streams shake out their character in a fascinatingly rapid succession from source to mouth. There are many such, some short and steep like the Etive, others, like the upper Tay, too long for a single or a safe day, for they show their teeth with gradually increasing strength as the swimmer himself begins to tire. For the long ones, a terrestrial friend is needed, to set camp ready for you in the evening by some shingle bank among the haughs, to whose glow you bump wearily across shallowing pebbles trying vaguely to remember which mental command should tauten the haunch muscles and raise you trembling to the semi-vertical once more. Three or four camps can serve the longer rivers, but the lower stretches of these—like the Welsh Dee or the Tay—are badly polluted and unhealthy to swim through. One has this last difficulty throughout the lowland rivers.

With mountain rivers the great difficulty is to catch them just nicely plump, between drought and spate. If too lean, you are always scraping aground or having to stagger through end-less shallows (and it is better to try and scrape than to stagger: repeated risings-up to wade are wearisome); if too full, then you tend to enjoy the memory more than the somewhat anxious experience. Usually, however, at least one consider-able stretch of a river is in condition.

Lakes offer quiet touring, and a circuit can occupy several days. Unless the lake possesses particularly varied scenery, one or two days is enough. There is no lure of the unknown in lakes as in the endless unwinding sea coast, and pursuing a lake-shore for its own sake (as distinct from exploring or lounging in the lake water) becomes after a day or so recogniz-ably akin to a dog chasing its tail, and no climax, no summit, is ever attained: merely the place you set out from. A sea loch is much better, for it can be followed, river-like, to the open sea and the final broadening-out to ocean is a goal well worth several days of journeying.

This meeting with the final sea is after all the great lure of river travel. Yet one of the finest of such experiences occurred to me not with a river nor even a sea loch but with that sheltered Linn of Lorne which, lying between Benderloch and Lismore, appears almost closed at the north end and opens irresistibly to the south. Here the whole topography enhances the final reward. I mention it now because like a river tour it had a real ending; tours in the sea itself have no ending—the horizon always coaxes you onward.

I started off below Loch Creran and followed the mainland shore southward. On my right, across the smooth lake of sea, Lismore lay at anchor, uncannily green and flat. Beyond it rose the hills of Morvern, mounting ever higher behind me to the culmination of Ardgour and the piled summits of Glencoe. Dark clouds passed over these background peaks and sheets of fine rain hid them intermittently. They continued on my left, vanishing down towards Beinn Starav, behind the rocky coast-line I was following. This coastline slanted dead straight down towards the sun-glitter in the south-west, where small clouds played across a clear blue sky. My objective lay there, the final skerries off the last finger of Fionn Ard, shining impossible miles away and pointing into the open sea-way between Mull and Kerrera.

I kept close to the shore rocks, which fell unbroken beneath the surface for twenty feet or so and then tilted out steeply to darkness. I drove on steadily, over the unrolling laminarian depths, allowing the distance to pass numbly by, soothing in its monotony. Obediently the great hump of Eilean Dubh backed out of sight on my right hand. Ridges of scrub oak came in at my left and accompanied me each a little way, one after the other. Small bays appeared between them and were passed, their charms ignored. That southern gateway called too strongly.

The tide was against me now, for I had to return this way and trusted to ride back on the inflow. I kept closer in to the rocks, desperately hoping each black finger ahead was the final point. But as I rounded each, another and another slid out and blocked the view. Surely I should give up; but I remembered mountain ridges like this, and how the summit always did appear just when it was quite impossible to persuade oneself to go further. And I was gaining height: Lismore itself was dropping behind me, farm after farm, and the small cluster of islets in the open sea—Eilean na Cloiche, Pladda and the rest—rose ahead larger and larger. Yet another interminable bay, black water beneath. Black rocks on my left, bent sea-birch on their skylines, and behind me sweeping veils of rain. Useless to go on—another hour at least, and the backs of my legs were becoming rubbed by the neoprene. Oh, to drift back on the blissful tide. . . .

And then into sunshine and ease. The last point fell away as dramatically as does every summit slope. There was nothing between me and the great south-western sea. A cool wind played on my face as I raised the mask. Lismore disappeared on my right into a cluster of islets and a terminal lighthouse; on my left the coast retired eastward into a soft bay tumultuous with oakwoods and sunlight, its fields pricked with hay-cocks. I paddled myself forward with exquisitely deliberate strokes and hauled out on to the last flat, sun-warmed skerry; its two or three gulls flapped away.

I had an astonishing view, and an astonishing backdrop. Great hills almost encircled us—from Cruachan and Starav on the one side, right round behind me under the storm clouds to the final flourish of Morvern over there on my right and the huge blue mountains of Mull. In front lay Kerrera and the last cliffs of Mull, with the ocean brilliant between them. Dotted in its farthest distance, the tips of the Garvellachs. After the hours of constriction this great expanse of waves and light was intoxicating.

I lay there in the sun for a long while, level with the murmuring weed; until the wavelets licked right over the edge of my platform. If I were to use the tide I had to be leaving. So I slid into the dark water and kicked slowly away on the current, back towards the shadows and the cloud, very well contented. Such was one, unforgettable, meeting with the sea.

But we must keep to the subject of this chapter and meet the sea from higher up, from well up in the land, so that the contrast shall be even greater.

Let us take an imaginary river, then, and make our way to its banks high in the heather some bright late-September morning, far above the last gaunt and coppered rowan. We had a good breakfast about an hour ago and have arranged for sandwiches some three hours downstream, and a good

E

congratulatory hot meal at the tent beside the ultimate sea loch: which we should easily reach—even with sun-lounging —before dusk.

Only a pedant would search out the actual source, and then wade dutifully down the infant miles; one does not usually climb every mountain from high-water mark.... The first driftable pool will suit, and thereafter one must guide and push, threading the boulders in six inches of scurry, elbowing over rock sills, plunging into gathered pools, noting how the force grows ampler, the banks more defensive. Soon there is no question of pulling through the rocks—one has to stave them off, must plot ahead the course both under and above the surface, and be always ready to kick aside from the sudden acceleration that may be the first warning of a steep water-slide or even a sheer drop; here one's interpretation of the banks ahead becomes valuable (for in rivers we know that land is as important as the water) and experience can soon foretell the approach of a region of cascades. The early ones can be slid down, feet foremost, arms braking on mossy boulders, but the stronger falls—spray rising mistily above them between leading walls of rock—have to be climbed down carefully, facing inward or sideways (fins are not as clumsy for this as you might think—their flat surface grips remarkably well); after such drenching ladder-work it is wonderfully relaxing to fall sideways into the dark pool below and feel oneself lifted up safely while the rock plunges on beneath the surface, and to be carried round the pool once or twice before launching out again with the restless waters.

After the steeper falls, some of which require a clambering descent down the banks themselves, the rocks under the cascade being too overhanging or obscured, after the release of these high waters, the river moves on more slowly for a while, satisfied, between high quays of rock peopled with colouring autumn trees. Gold and copper leaves drift with you on the black surface among crumbs of cream froth, with the odd travelling cluster of scarlet berries. The quietness is welcome; only here and there along the edges does a hiss in some con-cavity remind you of the power running beneath.

Where the sun lights these canyons its beams pick out the shadowed pot-holes in the river bed. It is strangely disturbing to move out directly over these sudden black chasms; you feel the giddiness of height, the beckoning of vertigo: and then you have moved on, the reassuring golden rock basks below, plate on tilted plate—until the next drop slides into view. After several flights one becomes drowsily nonchalant, as in those dreams of effortless gigantic leaps, and only the scarcely perceptible increase of speed and rumble, together with a dipping horizon and a fog of spray, wakens one to the approach of the next cataract.

Is it a cataract, or only a swift whistle through boulders, foam-padded and possible? As you are not slaloming down familiar rapids with hard hat and pneumatic pillow but exploring sensitively, you move across to one of the rocky banks and use it as a brake, allowing yourself to be plucked cautiously from one released handhold to the next, fins at the ready for a saving backward kick. This is agreeable rock-climbing for the lazy, a dream-like hand-traverse quite without effort, feet floating horizontally before you. A few yards more, and you can hook an arm round a large projecting flake and look down the steepening water to the hazard ahead.

It is only a chute, fat and safe, into a plump waltzing pool and you can cast off, accelerate madly into a whirl and explosion of spray, and emerge, head-shaking and buoyant, in the sleek lower waters and so put your face downstream again . . .

There comes a time when the river frankly enters a flatter course, rolling with greater power and importance between more subdued banks, only here and there breaking into a snarl over shelves and bouldery declivities. If managed happily, the break for a meal would come just before this change, and be taken on springy turf, feet still trailing into the current—for actual severance from all water is almost a physical shock, an amputation, after a morning tuned to the sea-rush; lying and eating is curious enough, ears still ringing with the journey, hands sodden with water now far ahead of you. A light meal, a rest, and within an hour one can slip back and be borne along once more, snug under the travelling counterpane, the unnatural incident forgotten.

These flatter waters are more restful, but no highland river is for dozing in. Hands and eyes must always be ready for boulders or spars, or wire thrown in from fields, or for sudden scooped places at sharp bends or constrictions—especially by the rare bridges—where a down-suck may lie in ambush so that you have to kick out strongly, emerging yards downstream, blinking in surprise. But there is no savagery in these rivers out of spate and their powerful middle courses are safe enough if you keep awake for a flip out of trouble, like the last man scrambling down a loose ridge with his rope poised for belays.

But finally, in a pour of relief the river surges on to its last dark flatness, and rocks and banks drop behind; low fields and marshes take over, and heavy-headed alders and willow. The water loses interest in you, gathers itself deeper below, its surface slower and more preoccupied. Probably, if you have judged well, the evening is beginning and the promise of sea is lying out between the great flanking peaks, at the sun-glitter. You are almost there. Below each bank, leaves of water-grass strain to seaward; shore winds buffet the rushes.

And then after the next swung bend the urgency eases, the current finally slips aside and you drift soundlessly towards the new water out there grey and ruffled between the black mountains, the lax banks disclaiming all responsibility now, folding back and disappearing; whalebacks of mud sniff by, ample acres of pebbles obtrude. You turn over and gaze back up the glen, beyond the twist of trees and over the gapped rocks that mark the climbing watercourse, back to the far moorlands where both your day and the river began. But the new currents are taking over, the view swivels round, cold water slaps your face, the small bucketings of sea waves begin to shake you. It is time to find the tent out there on the shore. With new firm deep-water strokes you coast along the delta, enjoying after those tumultuous hours the unimaginable ease of space, of breadth as well as length, and of water no longer obsessed but content simply to be. Water stretching out beyond the opening sea loch to the Atlantic, to the Caribbean, to grey Labrador: a shudder of vastness. There are many resounding analogies for this final emptying of a river into the amplitude of sea, ranging from Beethoven through the sexual orgasm to death itself. You may pick your own; but be sure to gather the experience, for a river must be swum to its conclusion, as a mountain be climbed to its summit.

Sometimes the last stretches are longer. Like those undecided hills that delay their final cairn by a succession of subsidiary tops, the slow tidal rivers unwind for hours to a sea always just round the next bend. Yet such places, too, must be known, for they are the fulfilment of rivers, sown at the source, immanent in the first spring water over its moss. These final stretches, piercing with gull-call and washed in monochrome, their marram grass pale in the wind beneath grey clouds, their dull water circling and muddy, fingering the odd birch and alder leaf, their small eddies deafened by the cold boom of waves across the distant sand-bars—these are best recalled by the closing paragraphs of *Anna Livia Plurabelle*, surely—for the author was reckoned by Jung to be no mean diver—the richest evocation of a closing river-day.

# 11

## *About touring in the sea*

And so we have returned to the sea. How should we best describe sea-touring? Again, I believe, by outlining a typical tour; not any trip in particular, but one assembled from many excursions along a broken, islanded coastline, preferably in the west. Western, because apart from the (at present) greater likelihood of oil-fouling off the eastern coasts from ships and wells, their sandy shores possess a monotony haunting to experience but not to read about. This monotony is at times liable to gross interruption, as when your course intercepts a procession of untreated sewage from one of the cities. Such migrations can occupy a band remarkably narrow —often only a few yards between the outriders on either side —but of great length, and possess a melancholy dignity of their own as they are shepherded out towards (one hopes) oblivion by the relentless tides. Crossing under this traffic requires a cool head. These transitory excitements apart, the east coast holds nothing that the west coast cannot offer to a greater degree.

Yet one exception might be the great cliffs of Old Red Sandstone such as those that outcrop along the edges of Kincardine and Aberdeenshire. Settled weather calls for a trip below these monsters, so tall, level-topped and, even after they have been punished to isolated stacks or frank unshored collapse, so notably expressionless. One trolls with the huge green smearers at their feet, exploring judiciously a few of the long narrow *geos* that split them, riding in on a surge and backpedalling out again before being squeezed under suddenly-bared shelves of rock. Far above, the walls admit a slot of sky, but all about one heaves darkness, mutter and splash, as the tight-bedded sands face again, after so long, the returning sea. To escape from such echoing contraction to the blaze of sun and ripple of cloud shadow along red miles of cliff is delightful, and although we find little interest underwater the constant play of the green sea, and its occasional white irritation, round these impassive blocks is always satisfying; and there are unexpected bays, sun-exposed and with small waves dashing on pebbles, where someone, scrambling down slippery red earth and turf, can meet you with refreshment; caves, too, where enthusiasts might bivouac, like the one described by Hugh Miller on his similar Cromarty coast —but I have not tried them nor am likely to, for there is something unpredictable about North Sea waves and something too unyielding about these bare cliffs, and I remember the Bullers o Buchan in a storm. No, let us finish with the east coast by cruising in to the beach at one of its many small resorts, and drag ourselves up past the staring paddlers. At such landing places there is little seclusion and perhaps with pleasant irony one should pay to enter the outdoor swimming pool—carefully cemented away from the gusto of sea—and change to dryness in one of its dank little cabins.

At the west coast, then, on a fine summer morning, with route known and refreshment arranged; say some eight or so miles, allowing for five hours' easy swimming and two or three more for idling and feeding. As we walk down to the water, what perils can be thought of?

The main sources of danger, apart from failure of one's own stamina, are rip tides and predators. The first can be studied from the shore beforehand, or their likelihood estimated from map or coastal pilot. There are many places where rip currents off a headland or in narrows can be embarrassing; some possibly as fatal as the notorious Corrievreckan at certain combinations of moon and wind.

There is a desperate area off the end of Lismore where, when wind fights tide, the water leaps up in a thousand angry points—the *Buinne nam Biodag*—tide-race of the dirks; you do well to avoid such battles. The old language has many names for the lurking sea-treachery of this coast in bad weather; what more expressive than the *bristeadh bodha*?— that sudden surge over an unsuspected reef when one wave out of a slow sea gathers itself and breaks without warning, and out of its trough rises the crocodile back of the waiting rocks. Yet among surges and reefs you are probably better off than booted fishermen in rigid boats; you can, as I have described, even enjoy them. Rip currents are another matter.

Any I have met have been easily foreseen, either by scurrying of weed or debris under water—startling enough—or by that querulously broken surface, so different from healthy white water blown or sucked without counterpressures from beneath. Most I have avoided, shore-hugging; some—as at the neck of a sea loch at change of tide—I have crossed with no more trouble than a tingling scalp (but the distance was only a tempting hundred yards or so and driftwood ran past safely enough). The principle is, of course, never to fight a strong current, here any more than in rivers (and rivers give good practice), but to go along with it, conserving your energy and easing yourself always a little further from its centre until, as from a tedious arm-clutching acquaintance, you can slip away whenever opportunity presents the lee of a skerry or a headland; but gang warily, warily, for there is as yet no West Coast Pilot for swimmers, and some currents may go downwards, not along.... If your companion is whisked off by a sudden race as if by an avalanche, are you to follow him or stay clear and watch where he ends up? As in the hills, circumstances will dictate, but these possibilities, however remote, must be talked over together until the route is well known. They are, reassuringly, of negligible significance to any skilled swimmer with fins, suit and snorkel who keeps within calm shallow waters; and there are hundreds of miles of such shore in western Scotland or Ireland and long stretches in Wales and south-west England.

In case I am accused of confining myself to the northern country, let me recommend any stretch of the north coast of the Lleyn peninsula, from Aber Geirch below Edeyrn to Porth Colman; farther west, anything but calm weather makes one anxious and the end of the peninsula is certainly only for shore-cuddling. More restful waters return by Abersoch and a trip from there to Pwllheli—gentle beaches varied by the great cliff of Trwyn Llanbedrog, the blast of Llanbedrog sewage pipe and the ferns of Careg-y-Defaid—is very pleasant. The west coast of Anglesey, too—but let us keep to this Highland trip, for the discerning will all remember places to provide an afternoon's, or a day's, or two days', aquatic jaunt.

And of course searching for and plotting out such journeys from an Ordnance map is as enjoyable as planning a hill-walk. One soon learns to interpret the symbols, picture the warm blue, the dotted sands, the scarps, dunes, cliffs and overpowering headlands, to estimate tides and likely times, even smell the bog myrtle off long stretches of sea marsh; just as steep slopes, windy summits, boulderfields and feature-less plateaux can all be traversed on the unfolded paper in anticipation before, and in complacency after, an expedition over the mountains. Few things are more pleasant than relaxing in a warm sleeping bag, full of bread, cheese and hot soup, fins and mask and neoprene lying cold and rinsed in the night mist outside the tent, and going over again on a map the twists and coves of coast, the horizons and great blue gaps you knew a few hours previously in the bright salted daylight; and imagining the next day's trip up to that curious little estuary and the three intriguingly green and wood-infested islands lying off it—particularly the one with Camas nan Geall, which must be a wide beach, sandy among weeded boulders at low tide, silverweed strewn among the white pebbles. . . .

The most intricate map-tracking involves a traverse of Ben-becula or the Uists. One starts in the sullen Minch, say at Rudha nam Pleac, and works in past Loch Maddy, getting tanglier and muddier, over to the clean peat-water mazes of Lochs Skealtar and Scadavay, among gneiss and flag-irises; a tent has been pitched somewhere there, and next day you try to break west to Loch nan Geirsann and the great sands opposite Berneray, stalking the fierce tides out to the bright Atlantic. . . . No maps are more delightful than those of the water-threaded Outer Hebrides.

We had mentioned predators. Predators only become credible once the bottom has sunk out of sight and one is crossing that naked bay to the far headland. The bay opens stark to the southwest and the sun exposes it unmercifully. The Atlantic is underneath. Shores are thin and distant and no help whatever. Were one walking, one's knees would start to tremble; as it is, they flex dutifully, but with lessening conviction.

The really blood-curdling, knee-dissolving predator, our own super-shark, is *Orchinus orca*, the killer whale. It usually hunts in small packs, is vicious-minded and is supposed to be alarmingly numerous off the West Highland coast, sometimes being found high and dry on the shore, rammed there by excess of enthusiasm, while around it are reputed to lie the tumbled bodies it pursued—stranded in terror seconds before it—seals, dolphins, fish of all kinds. I have never met one, which is presumably why I am able to write this, but the danger signal is, I believe, the sight of seals lying hauled well up on their rocks and islands, waiting until the pack moves on. So I am reassured at the start of a trip by the confident bobbing of black heads out in the bay; *they* would know.

In the bay, however, they themselves provoke tickles up the spine. Seals are so damnably competent. I have tried, on such a trip as this, to photograph them, challenging the nearest foolishly amiable face to a mutual dive. Down I would go, smoothly self-assured, perfect in control, knife sharp at my side (just in case), camera poised; and when I saw that huge pale bobbin, its silk fur spun with bubbles, flash past at immense speed yet at the same time rotating slowly and lazily eyeing me, wearily moving its hind flippers, when I saw those hundreds of thousands of years of experience I realized what a pathetic spidery creature I was. Spluttering on the surface I knew without looking round that a black head was regarding me, contentedly quizzical, a few yards behind.

I managed to approach one head quite closely, once. Seals' heads sit remarkably still; this one watched me calmly from about twelve feet, water lapping just below nostril level, while I trembled with concentration and tried to estimate lighting and adjust the focusing knob. I have called to seals from boats and attracted them, even regaled them with the pipes while they closed in, round-eyed and appreciative: so I tried to entertain the head with *whoo hoo* and similar noises. Beneath its grave gaze I felt like a hack photographer with black hood and birdie-box patter confronting a far-too-intelligent child. *Whoo hoo*, indeed. My sitter may have been insulted, bored or even possibly frightened when I at last levelled the camera: but its head rose right out to the shoulders, there was a hiss—and the animal disappeared. It went under with a great splash, which was unusual, and a second later so did I—feet up and head down to see if any attack was being prepared: but there was no sign underwater. Rather shaken, I slipped back the lens cover and turned for the shore. Needless to say, the head had reappeared, some twenty feet away. I shall require a telephoto lens; or a more extensive vocabulary.

Out in the bay among several such pensive heads one feels at first like a small boy crossing a farmyard of dogs: do not show fright, hum a little, do not look round, sweat imperceptibly. One awaits the snuffle at the heels, the first exploratory nip. Seals have powerful jaws; I lay on a sandbank once watching one break up a huge salmon, a fish as thick as my leg. But they are peaceable beasts, pleasantly inquisitive, and enjoy visits from oddities. Even when you become used to them, you pass through their groups like an over-equipped tourist, dangling with sun-glasses, sun-hat, walking stick and enormous boots, who slips embarrassedly across the mild amusement of a village square among the mountains.

Perhaps, however, they are not aware of one's incompetence; they certainly flee from good thwacks of the fins on the water surface. My only qualms with the common seal concern being mistaken at the time of rut for a competing male or, later, as a potential devourer of the pups; but I imagine that the aggressive display evoked would give me ample warning. The Atlantic seal might be a more difficult companion; he eyes a canoe balefully enough. I don't think I would trouble him for a photograph.

Other beasts may be met, but they are hardly potential predators. Sea-faring otters are common, slithering rat-like over the tangle, bounding hooped like a stoat among the rocks and then—plop!—only a small black head swimming vigorously away from you into the dusk. Cattle and horses, especially in the Islands, are free on the beaches. You may see cows standing up to their bellies in the shallow bays or find them pacing you along the white sands, their bull out in the lead. Perhaps you may even see the *crodh-mara*, the real sea-cattle, wending their way home beneath the waves with a sea-maiden loitering behind, driving them in. The land-cattle themselves can wander remarkably far among the rocks. I had rounded one point near Appin and was hauling myself up for a brief rest on a tide-washed platform, sighing deeply, for this turning had been a long time coming. My sigh of relief on this ultimate rock was answered by a blast of air as if from a monstrous bellows. I looked up expecting to see something like the *cìrean-cròin*, the great sea serpent that requires seven whales for each meal, and gazed on the chewing and satisfied visage of a huge Highland heifer, yellow seaweed hanging from her muzzle. But she might well have been from the *crodh-mara*.

And once—once—I was nearly embroiled with a dog. Passing a beach with a few strollers on it, I noticed a dog, a large black one, swimming out to me. I hesitated, thinking of a photograph or at any rate of an amusing encounter. The dog was a very fast swimmer and came at me hungrily with jaws open, waves or no waves. I realized that he was in earnest. He was a beach-trained beast, skilled at grabbing and fetching back the biggest of flung sticks—and what was my snorkel but another and very special stick? My fins doused his enthusiasm as I fled from what could have been an undignified and alarming incident....

For a brief outline of a tour, then, we could begin by wading one bright morning into a narrow inlet, over shallow mud and pebbles, through limp fleets of wrack; and then we would push forward on to the ebbing tide with that luxury of slowness which comes from fresh muscles with a whole day before them. As on a long hill walk, a slow starting pace is best, with as few pauses as possible; later will come excuses for drifting and admiring the view, but until a good distance has been covered rhythm is all-important. Haste in the sea is even more out of place than in a river; the scale is too vast, an extra greedy knot an impertinence.

Farther out, where the enclosing arms of rock slide back, the waves bounce in a light sea wind. Bobbing among them are yellow globes marking lobster pots; gazing below, you see the anchoring ropes furred and streamered, leaning with the tide. On diving down, the terminal pot emerges painfully from green shadow, usually at a chest-breaking depth. I have seen occupants a few times—as a plaintive feeler or a disconsolate hump—but never poked further, for as well as being uncomfortably far down one feels that either from the shore or from a puttering boat that will inevitably just be rounding the point lobstermen are watching with understandable suspicion.

At these depths the sea floor is only for occasional visiting by the snorkel swimmer, and morning is the time to cover distance; so along with the ebb one strikes away from familiar haunts and follows down the coast. The strength of tides I have mentioned before; if the bottom with its weed-pointers is invisible, then taking sights on landmarks during a few minutes' drifting will inform you how strong a correction has to be made. To cut across the opening of the next wide bay you make for its opposite shore, when the emptying water will take you far enough out just to miss the last seaward point of land, where waves whiten the rocks; approaching this promontory you feel the flush beneath you and steer accordingly.

Not far from the rocks black heads are watching, and as you pass they assemble respectfully before and behind. Lying flat, with fins still, you are carried right up to one, watch the pooled eyes and the water slapping the rubbery muzzle, the dripping whiskers; and then silently the owner has turned over and vanished, and you instinctively curl up your legs.

The water is fairly wild at the point and you must decide whether to clear it completely, allowing yourself to be carried to darker water well beyond, or whether just to creep round the inshore rocks. Those barnacled slabs heave unpleasantly, and although the tide runs quite fast off the point, the wind is falling, the day just begun and the coastline known to be safe; besides, you long to wrestle those offshore waves, to cream their plump flanks. So you beat out into the brilliant spray and salt, the sting of sudden air, the drench of immersion.

As the Gaelic has precise names for every shape of hill on the land, from the sharp *sgùrr* through *beinn* to the rounder *meall* and the smooth *monadh*, so it has for these bewildering hills of the ocean, equally familiar to the old people and celebrated in their magnificent sea-poetry; but the terminology is beyond my small skill in the language. Clearly, though, off this point the journeying roll of the *tonn* is giving way to the sharp *stuagh*, poised in its leap before breaking. And it is into the jumble of the *stuaigh* that you drive now.

The waves rear up, there is a good elbow-plunging ascent; then they slump onward and you slither down their backs, fins meeting air behind you at the passing crest. The valley you enter is ominously quiet, its shaking water circled with foam, and from here the next range of waves looks enormous, capped with tottering white water; but in no time at all a swimmer is high on their ridges and sliding downhill into another receiving glen. Occasionally one creamer spills its avalanche in your face; as if climbing a gully through a spindrift of powder snow, you shake your head through the dazzling spray and haul out on to the crest. Looking round, one sees roll after roll of them, white hair streaming down their backs, racing to the black point and exploding there in tall columns; clouds of spray punctuate the coast, showering down slowly in the wind. Then all is hidden by the shoulders of the last battalion and the penalty for not keeping eyes ahead is a heavy blow on the mask as the next breaker, the *éiseanach*, the high following one, collapses on you in the valley. When rhythm is lost in a mishap like this one can be swept back a dozen yards struggling in the water-slide and under-suck; on such occasions I blow clear and then dive straight under the next wave, surfacing about its shoulder-blades, blowing again and making good speed into the dip; a few such dives, if not any faster than surface swimming, restore one's equanimity. Farther out, the valleys are wider and the oncoming mountains, though linked shoulder to shoulder with separate peaks appearing and disappearing like heads in a manoeuvring rugby scrum, offer clear lines of ascent; one has time to plot a green-water crossing.

At last, safely away from the shore-fighting, you twist on to your back, relax, and allow yourself to be pulled out past the snout of rocks, watching them spin away at astonishing speed. The water does the work now and breath can be gasped again as you are borne away, rising and falling, on the green roller-coasters; they have changed themselves back to the more purposeful *tonnan*.

Round the point, although some hundreds of yards out from land, you are, as forecast, in less agitated water and able progressively to move inwards again. Rising and bundling forward among the schools of waves in the bright morning sun is delightful, and you watch the unrolling shoreline in detachment; you have no wood, no oars, no sail or motor to worry about, to ship, heave or tinker with. Free with the ocean, the sky and the wind, you notice houses come into sight every so often, outbuildings, a shack, all perched high and dry on bare gneiss above the white rollers, Norwegian-like; and then they pass out of view and are banished from the mind as the scene changes and the land folds back and sinks, and the flat estuary of a river appears.

The thin beach, whitened by sand-bars, is almost invisible and surely you are far enough out, even though the shore will move to meet you at another promontory an hour or so ahead.... Then, between the swish and roar of waves, which even here are four or five feet from trough to crest, stutters the unmistakable note of an engine, and you lie back and kick white pointers to your position. The boat passes, on its way from the estuary, some twenty yards ahead, its crew of two standing in surprise; then it vanishes for ever, engulfed by the waves, its staccatto exhaust surging once or twice before extinction.

Boats are often encountered when touring, and they can be quite useful. I had once swum half an hour out from a Fife village when I looked down and discovered that my knife and its sheath had slipped off. Assuming I had subconsciously noted the loss as it occurred, I turned back and, sure enough, within a few yards saw the yellow cork handle of the knife bobbing among the small waves. Below it, the blade stuck wickedly down (it is always perilous hunting for a floating knife) and there was no sign of the sheath. The sheath was a poor one—which was why it had slipped off—but I valued the knife. However, a knife without a sheath is a liability afloat. I certainly was not going to stuff it beneath the belt sheathless; one incautious double-bend would introduce the first movement of *hara-kiri*. Nor would I tow it behind, for it was razor-edged and once caught among my leg strokes ... moreover, one would never feel a gash in the water until too late. Either I had to carry it in one hand and thereby lose all flexibility in swimming, or I had to return. I was preparing, with much annoyance, to return when I noticed a small boat being rowed rather inexpertly a little way off. In it were a man—obviously a genially-tweeded holidaymaker—and a girl about twelve. They were making for the harbour after fishing in the bay. I approached and hailed them courteously. One forgets terrestrial norms; touring swimmers are as yet unusual. The girl became, and remained, goggle-eyed but the oarsman, presumably her father, was a gentleman up to his gabardine fishing hat and resolutely evinced no surprise though obviously rather at a loss. When I asked if he would mind leaving this particular knife inside the spare wheel of a Land-Rover parked on the jetty, he seized on the relatively commonplace message with relief, nodded vigorously and, bending over to take the glittering weapon, managed a reasonable smile. Words, however, were still beyond him. He laid it carefully on the bilge boards among tangled fishing lines and I left them both sitting staring down at it; some minutes passed before he dipped his oars and resumed heaving homeward. On my return that evening I found the knife neatly tucked in the spare wheel.

There was another occasion, farther north on that east coast, when I was not so clever. I met a fishing vessel just off a promontory; it was obviously heading out from a near-by village and cutting the last corner. Waves were fairly boisterous and the bucketing boat would appear and disappear behind them, bow smacking up clouds of spray. The crew were pulling ropes and nets about on deck. Out of sheer thoughtless exuberance, instead of watching quietly I lay back and kicked high white water. This foolishness produced a startlingly immediate reaction. The crew, as I saw them between intermittent wave crests, jumped about and pointed excitedly. They had evidently seen me as well as my plume. To my consternation, the engines changed note; the boat was going to stop. One man stood on the wheelhouse and waved, the rest ran to the stern: perhaps they were going to cast off in a dinghy—I could not see.

This was very bad. Here were decent men, not only stopping in the middle of a hard-enough job, but stopping in a rough sea by a rocky headland and perhaps risking their lives further by setting out in a small boat (for as fishermen they would not be able to swim)—all because of a moment's aberration. Fortunately I did not wave back; also, I was wearing a hood. The heaving waves obscured vision. Perhaps they might think it had been a seal or something like that, after all, if I disappeared at once; to swim up and apologize would surely do nobody any good and even if I escaped being brained by a righteously indignant oar, heaven knows what ill omens they would collect from this adventure—they who dare not meet a red-haired woman or a minister before setting out; I might even pronounce, in my confusion, tabu words like 'rabbit' or 'salmon'— was 'seal' equally unmentionable? So I dived, without flaunting fins, and swam shorewards until nearly bursting; then I surfaced, tried to look as much like a seal as possible, and dived once more. When, exhausted, I reached heavy waters by the headland itself I risked peering again. The vessel was still there but, thank goodness, there was no sign, in that lurching sea, of a dinghy, and the crew seemed gathered in a knot; two were on the wheelhouse but, as I watched, they dropped stiffly down. A series of white waves blinded me for a few minutes and when I could wipe my streaming mask again, the boat was clearly moving away; but the men were still standing in a group, watching the coast. There would be tales, perhaps, of selchies that night.

I have often wondered if the visions of those claiming to have seen selchies—seal-people who came out of the sea on moonlit nights, took off their seal skins and danced round them on the shore—were not a form of the second sight, and what they told of will eventually come to pass when more people are swimming freely off our coasts. I can imagine few things more pleasurable, in a suitably permissive society, than youths and girls swimming ashore, stripping off their neoprene, and dancing together in the moonlight. Wet-suits may make Polynesians of us all.

Can the same phenomenon explain *an t-each uisge*, the notorious 'water-horse'? This terror of young maidens would emerge from loch or sea in the likeness of a man and make dangerous love; if you noticed, in time, the seaweed in his hair, and fled, you were safe; otherwise . . . and then he took you back to the water with him. I have swum in one Loch an t-Eich Uisge (and there are many), whose name suggests occupancy by such a clammy gallant, and possibly my dripping emergence that evening may have been foreseen long ago by some talented prophet; but as I have never yet encountered in such places any local maidens (they having all been driven to Glasgow or North America) we must presume the seer added on the last bit as self-indulgence. Still, he may have been correct; I shall possibly pass that way again, and one never knows one's fortune in these matters. . . . But it is high time to return to our original and wholly respectable sea tour.

Not least among the joys of a swimming trip is the chance at any time to vary your strokes and position; it is as if you could walk or run sideways or backwards, on hands or knees or feet, or be carried effortlessly forward on one foot or one hand or on none at all. For much of this trip you have been idling, borne by waves and tide and hardly exerting yourself, relying simply on continuous gentle pedalling with your legs, your arms hanging limp or folded, so now you feel a little chilled and an urge for exercise. Therefore, sighting carefully landward of the next rocky headland, you thresh forward into a crawl, raising your eyes regularly to keep course, which—as we observed earlier—is difficult with no visible sea bed to steer by. Down below is nothing but travelling greenness, grains and suspended fragments pouring past beneath you as you strive, slowing as you relax. A dive takes you down through formless translucency, with no hint of sea floor even when the darkness comes up and squeezes your ribs. Rising, you loll sideways and watch the surface fluttering down towards you; then you roll on to your belly, blow out the water and drink in the air, and stroke forward again with your arms, driving them in that precise unhurried rhythm which is so tireless and satisfying and beside which even the most accomplished striding of a *langlauf* skier appears jerky and contrived. You may bring your arms firmly out of the water and dive the fingers sharply in front of you; or cast arms loosely ahead and cup the hands. You can pass your arms right beneath and behind you like a canoeist's follow-through, or give up half-way, drifting them to the surface. Or, still continuing the loose-kneed kick, you may row yourself forward with the arm movements of the breast stroke: you progress then in slow rhythmic bursts as if wielding oars and fall naturally into the hypnotic refrains of the old rowing songs of these waters.

*Iomairibh eutrom ho-o ro....*

Form of stroke, time, and power exerted, all may be varied, and each variation gives its own pleasure, each conveys the particular response of the water. No wonder, then, you lose sense of direction and after several minutes of such swimming your eyes, when they do break the surface, see ahead of them not the aimed-for point but waves jostling to the empty horizon; and you have to swing back on course with strenuous pulls of one arm.

But you are now quite near the tall headland Sròn Ruadh, beyond which a friend is supposed to be waiting for you with food; as a further change of stroke you can swivel on to your back and use only the knee-bent leg-pedalling, with its restfully sonorous thump, and watch your wake lather away behind you across the bay. It is pleasant to recline with head flat on the sunny water, conscious only of the connecting rods working away aft. Of course, the snorkel must be out of your mouth and you can—though beware of a slipping strap—push your mask back on your forehead and drink in unrestricted air and sunlight while the fair-weather cumulus sails above you to the peaks of Moidart. Hands are best folded across the belt buckle. I have often found myself dozing in this position, yet still keeping up a good speed. Direction is easily held and one rarely gets clouted by a breaking wave but courses up and down over their hurrying backs. It is a fine stroke for open water.

As your unprotected head would be the first to hit an obstacle, you develop the necessary responses. Shorter waves arouse suspicions; stretching round, you see that the long neck of rock you were aiming for is quite close, and scores of barnacle-yellow boulders and wet heads of weed dot the waters ahead. The tide must be fully out.

These shallows are good to dive in, and perhaps you follow the point mostly beneath the surface, parting the golden forests and moving through their liberated bubbles with camera poised, searching the blue alley-ways for a cruising school of fish or the white flicker of a seal. You have travelled a fair distance—had you walked along the twisting coast you would still be far behind—and it is tempting to stay and rummage among the gurgling stems. But food calls more strongly; so you continue until, high on a rock-table just round the point, you see your friend. He sees you; and you meet on an amphibious shelf, he dangling down from above, you reclining sofa-wise below. The sun, now past high noon, bakes the neoprene to blissful levels.

This meeting with a terrestrial inhabitant, this eating of jam sandwiches and drinking of strangely sweet juice, is a good pivot for the day. Before it one has concentrated on covering distance, and has enjoyed surface pleasures much as from a boat although more intimately; afterwards there will be slow exploration, on an infilling tide, among small islands and sandy reaches, covering less than half the distance but being—or looking—most of the time underwater.

I am always surprised, at such dramatic meetings, by the uncouth rustling of terrestrial visitors. I elbow myself out into sun, oozing pools; they scratch carefully down, halted by the first mattress of weed. We have a barrier between us. If the visitor is himself a swimmer, we can converse; if not, any adjustment is too laborious and we exchange polite nothings: commendations of the jam, or advice on the un-screwing of bottles—curiously difficult for sea-whitened fingers.

There is nothing so distancing from everyday uncritical human life as this sea-touring. Even on the starkest of ice peaks you stand on the same earth, perform the same movements, as does Glasgow or Stockholm; but ten metres out in the Clyde or the Baltic, and the surrounding boatmen are strangers. This distancing enforces re-examination. In a world increasingly dominated, and endangered, by the obses-sive conceit of over-industrialized society, it is very necessary to strip that society down to its units and discover the essen-tial humility and nobility, still intact, of the isolated indivi-dual. And one of the best ways of doing this is to watch such an innocent unit clambering down to meet you from a shaky shore at noontide; and then to become one yourself in the evening, hurrying landward tired, cold and drenched with inexplicable visions. Our temporary industrial dictator-ship is an attempted escape from the world and humanity; as a restorative of the sanity of modern man and with it an acceptance of the dignity of his limitations, I know of no pursuit better than such naked sea-touring.

On mountains you are forever encountering summit cairns, old tracks, megalithic observatories or suchlike associative distractions; in a boat you have either its own personality intruding or those of the thousands before you who held the tiller or drove the oar. Swimming free you are liberated from any social framework and can examine your fellow men with rare objectivity. You see that one man slipping about on the rocks, so far from the road and his motor car, you see the smoke down-coast where thousands more endlessly count stones and throw them at the water: and so refreshing is the loss of contemporary obsessions that you are tempted to grow arrogant with the ocean and deny kinship with such creatures. But you know that if you put off your human existence this way and strike out in heartless ecstasy of living, biting through waves to other rocks and other islands among the rocketing shearwaters and the idle seals, out to the far sun-glitter—then you will incur the late tide and a cramping belly, the whimpering return, or no return. So you temper this exuberance, superhuman or infrahuman, with common sense and wake up from your sun-dreaming, take a last drain of the orange juice, thank your patient friend (whose shoes will never recover), confirm the evening's meeting place and, replete with food and gratitude, swirl and wallow away. You could not be here without your friend's help; nor can you, like the seal, grow your own neoprene. Always we live on the human knife-edge, in the precarious dignity of balance; and because, on land, we have temporarily lost sight of both our land and our sea, it is good to be here and discover them again from the broken coastal waters, with nothing underfoot but the first twenty fathoms of the Atlantic.

The remainder of the day is spent leisurely from rocky island to island, exploring below as we have described and occasionally, in the slow journey down the coast, moving out far from land; the slanting afternoon sun pours avenues under the waves and one may follow them a little before giving up and rising through a lightening green world to the fish-wandering surface. Joining together these illimitable vistas are weedy nodes of skerries, seen ahead orange through the haze, rooted far down in darkness, their skirts swaying. You nose up through their warm cluster and lie across the tangle in the sun. Perceptibly you are lifted higher off them by each travelling wave. The tide is obviously coming in quite fast. Shoulders of weed around you, planted on deeper reefs, are shrugging beneath the surface. The sea notably gathers force, so that to cling to the disappearing skerry one has to wrap the yellow thongs tightly round one's wrist, and face cold slaps of hurrying water.

Possibly at this time a dark cloud covers the sun and the rain shower, moving as a sheet from seaward, passes over you. If your head is bare, the surprisingly cold rain pelts your scalp, but otherwise you feel nothing. The shining sea-skin, though, is puckered and freckled all round you. Releasing hold, one may drift away in this downpour, land and horizon obliterated, waves fly-bitten and opaque. A dive restores normality; but on looking upwards, the surface is flickering with tiny dots.

On these moist summer evenings the mackerel or the cuddies may be leaping round the inner skerries. You see ahead, as you move inshore, an insistent bickering of spray unlike the usual slow and rhythmic drench of water over rocks; there is a faint crackling, a scaly whispering. It is best then to gaze along the surface, with vision both above and beneath; and one enters a mosquito cloud of fish, spiralling like birds below, spinning and slapping on the water above. The noise is of great wet grasshoppers in the hay. You may pass among them, their quick backs bounding rubberlike from legs and arms, their splashes streaming off the mask. On diving down and looking up you see this long quarrelling fringe of fish, like a line of unsettled starlings, stretching above the higher submarine rocks, powdered with bubbles. They are totally oblivious of you; and you leave them to their business, and continue with the waves towards the calmer waters inshore.

This way, lazily, without effort, one is rolled nearer the mouth of the sea loch chosen as landing point. In front, the hills are moulded orange against a darkening sky, their burns shadowed by the alder-clumps that wander up their flanks; behind you, the westering sun dazzles the water.

Underneath it is too dark to see much; the water feels colder and legs are beginning to tire.

Among the advantages of water-travelling are not only the instant rest achieved by merely relaxing the limbs (without a disturbing collapse on to bony ground) and the instant progress resumed by simply moving them again (without the wearisome clamber up on to teetering legs), but also—if you have planned well—the easy downhill run home on a fresh incoming tide, riding the strong haunches, cheered by their success. But of course if you have miscalculated then you face, as we noted earlier, a most uphill task in beating back through an ebbing tide, in dodging from skerry to skerry and cheating the races off headlands; evening, an empty belly and tired limbs make a poor business of what is otherwise an exhilarating game.

On the hills similar misjudgements incur benightment, when you may have to sit on a rock ledge or in a snow hole or behind some boulder until the unthinkably remote dawn. I have never been benighted at sea, nor would I recommend it; but with a wet-suit and emergency glucose the experience, though unpleasant, need not seem terminal. I should advise, as on a hill, staying put: seizing hold of some skerry or islet (likely on an ebb tide to remain dry all night) as an anchorage; seaward drift would be the enemy, or hitting an unseen rocky shore in high waves. Certainly it would seem best to reach a near-by island, even farther out, rather than to try and force an ebb tide to the coast itself. On bare shores it is more difficult. The solitary swimmer is, of course, asking for trouble; two can at least chivvy each other awake. All this inconvenience can, however, be easily avoided by coming in close to shore early—if you have to leave it at all—and on the flood tide.

Night swimming is, when deliberately sought, more pleasantly memorable. I have dived with a companion for lobsters off the West Highland coast in pitch darkness, wielding a rubber-covered torch. We found few lobsters, but the sensation was curious. On first swimming out I drank much invisible water before being able to bite the snorkel grip. Looking below, there was only the torch beam, and down its smoky path I had to venture. Rocks and weed were clear enough in the beam, but shadows were formidable, of absolute black and surrounded by a wavering penumbra. Around and, worse, *above* stood the same implacable darkness, resistant as a board. Fish blossomed brilliantly out of it; and, disappearing, were as abruptly extinguished. Such discontinuity emphasized the strangeness. I existed by virtue of Ever-ready or Vidor; I was no longer easy in the water. Most uneasy: an Atlantic-ful of monsters pressed against my small tent of light.

However, I dutifully poked about the winking bottom for lobsters and then, unwillingly, kicked off upwards into solid black, arms shielding my head. I broke surface with the torch, and breathed again.

I once dropped my light. It lay, a small white flower, about fifteen feet down. I found leaving the surface difficult because in the dark the only evidence of its existence was a tactile one; to achieve the correct diving position required much summoning up and examining of sensations. A wet-suit would make the problem worse. Another time, the torch went out when I was below. I couldn't find the vague under-rubber switch of these contraptions and anyway the bulb might have died or the casing leaked; so I dared not waste time fiddling but had to start immediately for where I hoped the surface lay. I had no wet-suit and not much remaining breath, and therefore possessed little buoyancy. But I had first to wait and make sure, by my buoyancy, which way *was* up. I could not, of course, see the essential bubbles; and my companion was somewhere round the point. Halfway 'up' I began to wonder somewhat; outstretched hands still met water, whereas I estimated I should have been by then several feet above the surface. I dreaded lest my 'up' had been in fact a horizontal current; a similar confusion, you may recall, can exist in the pale blue 'washout' of glacial lakes. But in such instances time is deceptive; I had actually been moving only a few seconds before my anxious fingers met, not the surface but its herald, the layer of warm upper water. Then they broke into cool night air, and I followed with considerable relief.

Cautious repeats of dark diving have not convinced me that it would ever be free of anxiety; as a stunt, it has its amusement. Let us leave submarine night to those better equipped: to the aqualung divers and their powerful apparatus—and their time for repairing it.

Night swimming—as distinct from diving—can be a wonderful experience. Pick preferably a clear late spring night off the west coast when the evening wind has died and the waves have quietened beyond the fringe of rocks. As you wade out, the water breaks into sprays of phosphorescence, the sea-fire, the *teine mara*, and your swimming loosens silver chains behind you; every finger scatters its jewels. Diamonds burn on the rumpled velvet and above you ripple oceans of stars. All is hushed but the unseen wash of small waves outside the reef. Between black headlands water and sky echo and intermingle. You lie there, fingering out your own constellations and gazing beyond Andromeda.

But we were finishing our tour, in the evening light. If the reader is a sea swimmer, he will know the incoming sensations; if he is not, he has come far enough through this book to guess them. The increasing warmth, the maternal infolding of headlands at the outer beaches; the uncanny reluctance of the swimmer to leave the water, to haul out on to weedy rock or pebbles or sand. The last turn round, in the last few inches of water, shoulders hard on the stones, to gaze westwards at the black islands, Skye or Rhum, Eigg or Canna, or the sky-floating Outer Isles, or maybe the hump of Bardsey, or Trevose Head and the Qules, silhouetted against smoking gold; to watch gilded water spill and wrinkle off the rubber; to stretch out weightless limbs, head bumping gently on the beach, and look for the first stars succeeding to the lemon sky.

After a day spent afloat the effort required to turn over, crawl out, unbuckle, unstrap and clamber up is unthinkable. Only the call of the friend watching for you, only his hands under your shoulders, wake you back to the land-life you left so long ago. He is a rude awakening; but he has a supper cooking and a tent up there on the turf, spoons, plates and a dry sleeping bag and other things like that. And if you don't fully appreciate their value, your belly does. So it's up and stagger, his arm round your waist, the sea draining reluctantly back down your neck, swelling your knees and pumping from your boots; up and back through the growing darkness to the small glow of the tent. There is a wonderful tang of fried spam.

And far out at the golden skerries the cuddies are leaping, leaping continually.

# 12
## About aquatic parks - the swimming pools of the future

At the beginning of this book we expressed dissatisfaction with the present-day swimming bath, and likened it to a gymnasium or games yard. We considered it too restricting to be the only place available in a built-up area for the thousands who were able to swim and who wished to use their skill in an interesting, exciting or relaxing way.

Now a few people in towns practise gymnastics or play squash or basketball as their sole exercise, but most of them take jaunts in the park, enjoying the colour, air and space and the feeling of uncemented earth stretching out and unrolling itself before their eyes and beneath their feet. Trees and shrubs prolong horizons, fountains and rockwork vary the foreground. Parks are rightly considered essential to relieve the frustration of today's urban life, and we judge a civilization by the imagination displayed in designing them.

Our own technically advanced civilization should be able to provide aquatic parks to supplement its present aquatic gymnasia, even if only in a future when production and employment are geared to improve our surroundings instead of using them as a battlefield.

This new kind of swimming pool could be indoor or outdoor, or both. If outdoor, the water would still be heated, as in the huge but wearisome pool at Moscow (interesting only when condensation freezes to confectionery on the seats and railings round it and when, swimming, one blows tunnels through the steam). Such an aquatic park, designed to capture something of wider waters, will offer as much variety as possible, above and below; for this is how terrestrial parks appeal, by giving us great lawns, woodland glades, formal parterres, mazes and waterside scenes—all, we know, contrived and artificial in the middle of a big city but none the less enjoyable for that. Because the medium is so different, variety in an aquatic park will cover a different range of experience—one with which readers of this book will be by now familiar: variation in colour, sound and texture, in velocity and temperature of the water, in its illumination and depth. There will be places for all to enjoy, learners, children, lovers, misanthropes and the sociable, the energetic or the lazy. Some restrictions and supervision there must be, but no more than are acceptable for the best terrestrial parks or bathing beaches.

If we enter such a pool of the future, we see that those constricting and slippery tiles have gone. The entire wettable surface, shores, banks and bottom, is covered with a tough resilient plastic, of subdued shades and textures— brown, grey, golds and slaty-blues, smooth to knobbly, rippled or indented. Most illumination is from beneath, lamps of various colours, intensity and width of beam being set underwater in walls or floor; overhead, stars and planets glow from the deep blue domes of the roof, which in one part shimmers with a procession of hues recalling the Northern Lights. The water area is irregular, with bays and inlets, peninsulas and connecting canals, and with the surface in some places surging into waves, in others running as a fast current, and elsewhere reflecting the ceiling stars unbroken. The banks slope occasionally to shores, and swimmers haul themselves out there to lounge on the ribbed resilient neoprene and sun themselves beneath infra-red lamps. Caves may exist, discreetly lit, for the romantic; tall rubbery cliffs occur and there are islands flat, humped or pointed. To aid diversity, water falls and sprays (warm or cold) from places high up in the walls, or enters racing down chutes; hidden lighting transforms this into jewelled movement, and air, cascading upwards from the floor as curtains or necklaces of bubbles, is similarly lit and tinted. Ribbons of plastic, swaying crimson, gold and green, divide the different areas like hedges or shrubberies and, as they part, reveal successive vistas of this frankly artificial but imaginative waterscape.

Through such a Byzantium the swimmers move, mostly

with mask and fins—for without them progress is fussier and vision incomplete—savouring the change of light and colour, and the water's response. There are stretches along which to sprint, pools for floating in lazily beneath warm showers, rubbery submerged arches under which to dive. Deeper regions, safely lit, provide for exploration and offer solitudes from which to survey the bubbling iridescence of these underwater grottoes. There are windows, too, set in the walls beneath the surface, for round the periphery of part of this pool runs lounge and café, and from their tables diners or loungers can watch the procession of swimmers and divers in a separate world. Other glass windows—guarded by transparent mesh—look from under the surface into huge aquaria and there, like animals or birds within subaerial parks, fenced off from the strolling swimmers but apparently with them part of the scene, fish glide among a filigree of water plants.

Such a construction is undisguisedly artificial and gains its effect by being so; the moods of the water are there, and colour and light. Treated as an abstract design by Burle Marx or as an extension of discreetly informal urban landscape, it must be very much more satisfying than today's shrill box of green water. There are no great technical difficulties to overcome; money and ingenuity now spent on various auto-catalytic examples of Parkinsonian economics could readily produce such bright oases in tomorrow's conurbations. Exercise and adventure would exist at hand, independent of daylight, weather or season; one would discover the delight of water itself and, excited by such a foretaste, would be prepared for the greater natural scenery waiting outside in the seas, lakes and rivers, and be willing to risk hardship and passing discouragement in the search for it.

# Index

(Figures in parentheses refer to illustrations – between pages 58 and 59)

153